CANADA'S MAGNIFICENT MARATHON: 40 YEARS RUNNING IN OTTAWA

Mark Sutcliffe

Great River Media

Library and Archives Canada Cataloguing in Publication

Sutcliffe, Mark, author
Canada's Magnificent Marathon: 40 years running in Ottawa / Mark Sutcliffe.

ISBN 978-0-9868242-4-1 (bound)

1. Ottawa Marathon--History. 2. Marathon running--
Ontario--Ottawa--History. I. Title.

GV1065.23.C3S88 2014 796.42'520971384 C2014-902343-X

Great River Media Inc.

Suite 500 – 250 City Centre Ave.

Ottawa, ON

K1R 6K7

www.greatriver.ca

Research and coordination: Sarah MacFadyen

Book design: Lisa Georges

Cover design: Halogen Marketing

Printed and bound in Canada

About the author

Looking for a bit of exercise, Mark Sutcliffe went jogging for 30 minutes in 1998. He soon discovered a passion for running that changed his life. Since his first half-marathon in 2003, he has participated in Ottawa Race Weekend nine times, including four Ottawa Marathons (he is pictured here after his first, in 2004). For more than 10 years he has been writing and broadcasting about running, including his first book, *Why I Run*. He is the founder of *iRun*, and is the host of the weekly iRun radio show and podcast.

When he is not running, Mark is a journalist and entrepreneur. He hosts a daily radio show on 580 CFRA, writes for the *Ottawa Citizen* and is the CEO of Great River Media, which published Canada's Magnificent Marathon. Mark lives a few metres from the Ottawa Marathon course with his wife Ginny and their children Erica, Jack, and Kate.

1991

Sponsors

Ottawa Race Weekend gratefully acknowledges the support of the following partners who sponsored *Canada's Magnificent Marathon.*

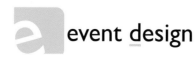

HOWARD SELCER & ASSOCIATES

2009

OTTAWA MARATHON | 2009

OTTAWA MARATHON | 2009
RED CORRAL
3708
ROB
• SUNDAY MAY 24, 2009 •

10502

Contents

One race, 100,000 stories

[PREFACE]

In 1984, Chris Worswick, my Grade 11 classmate at St. Pius X High School, announced he was planning to run the Ottawa Marathon.

It was my first direct exposure to the event. Until then, finishing a marathon seemed a superhuman feat, the metaphor for an elusive goal. I remember asking Chris dozens of questions about his training and his plans for the race. How far was a marathon? How long would it take him to finish? How often was he training? How fast did he run?

After Chris successfully completed the race and answered even more of my questions, I briefly pictured myself striving toward the same goal and finding out whether I had what it took to run a marathon. I even tried running a couple of times, but like most teenagers, I had neither the persistence nor the attention span for marathon training, and I soon gave up.

Five years later, I was covering the Ottawa Marathon as a young radio reporter. A photo of me approaching winner Gord Christie, microphone in hand, appeared on the front page of the *Ottawa Citizen*. Once again I was intrigued and even inspired, and briefly considered training for the following year's event. But it never moved from idea to action.

It wasn't until 2004, 20 years after my introduction to the marathon through my high-school friend, that I attempted the distance myself. As it was for Chris and so many other runners before and since, it was a life-changing experience. Like all worthwhile challenges, the marathon is equally difficult and empowering.

As an event, the Ottawa Marathon has become enormously successful. It's a remarkable annual tradition, a tourist attraction, and an enormous fundraiser for important causes like the Ottawa Hospital Foundation. As an increasingly popular community activity, it is a collective endeavour. There is no question that a runner feeds off the energy of the crowds of people in the race and alongside it. At the start line, we are all in it together.

But it is also intensely personal. No matter how much inspiration and support might fuel your effort, you are carried by nothing other than your own power from the beginning of your training to the end of the race. And during those long, final five or six kilometres before the finish line, the marathon runner often becomes very introspective. This is the part of the race during which you have a chance to learn something about yourself.

So in setting out to record the history of the Ottawa Marathon, I soon discovered that it wasn't one story, but thousands of them. What follows is an attempt to present a historical account of one event by capturing the experiences of some of the almost 100,000 people who have crossed the Ottawa finish line since 1975.

In the pages ahead, I hope you'll discover, as I did, that while across the years as well as the kilometres many things change, one remains constant. The journey of a marathon runner is inspiring and worthy, and there is great satisfaction in getting from the start to the finish – particularly at a spectacular, well-organized event like the Ottawa Marathon – one step at a time.

1976

"Why don't we put on a marathon in Ottawa?"

Canada's Magnificent Marathon

[INTRODUCTION]

In the early 1970s, Ottawa was home to a small-but-dedicated group of long-distance runners. Some of them trained together, others ran alone, passing each other on popular routes like the path next to the Rideau Canal.

For many of them, it was simply a way to get some exercise and spend time outdoors. But a few of the more passionate and ambitious runners in Ottawa trained for the ultimate endurance test: the marathon.

Inspired by a Robert Browning poem on the legend of the Greek messenger Pheidippides, the organizers of the first modern Olympics had created the marathon three-quarters of a century earlier, in 1896. The following year, the Boston Marathon was launched. And early in the 20th century, sparked by the exploits of 1908 Olympic champion Johnny Hayes and 1907 Boston winner Tom Longboat, there was a brief period running historians refer to as "marathon mania," with races featuring anywhere from a dozen to more than a hundred participants sprouting up here and there across North America.

But other than the Boston Marathon, few events survived that fleeting interest in long-distance running prior to the Great War. In the 1950s and 1960s, there was barely more than a handful of small amateur races across North America. The New York City Marathon was launched in 1970, but unlike at future editions, when a lottery would be required to choose participants, only 55 runners crossed the finish line the first year.

Interest in long-distance running soon began to grow again after Frank Shorter became the first American since Hayes to win the Olympic Marathon in 1972. And as the marathon became more popular, and a few more races appeared on the calendar, runners from Ottawa began to travel to Boston and other destinations in the U.S. to fulfill their goals.

"A bunch of us were bumping into each other at marathons," says Ken Parker. "It caused a few of us to start thinking about whether we should have our own race."

"It was expensive to travel to Boston and other races in the U.S.," says Bill Williams. "After a while, somebody said, 'Why don't we put on a marathon in Ottawa?'"

Parker, Williams, and a few other Ottawa runners met with city officials in the summer of 1974. A route was planned, starting and finishing at Carleton University, where a sports medicine clinic had recently been launched by one of the marathon volunteers, Dr. Don Johnson.

On May 25, 1975, a warm, sunny day, the first Ottawa Marathon was run. A total of 146 runners crossed the finish line, led by Mehdi Jaouhar, who finished in 2:26:39. Compared to more recent participation numbers, that's a small field. But in 1975, that was the largest marathon in Canada.

Parker says the key to the event in its early years was the fact that it was organized by runners. "We had a tag line: the runner's race," he says. "We had all marathoners on the race committee."

That meant special attention was paid to the small details that would matter to participants, like having the course certified and making sure that water stations had cups that were suitable for runners. That respect for runners not only attracted a growing number of amateur participants, but it set the stage for Ottawa to host two important national qualifying races – for the 1976 Olympic team and the 1978 Commonwealth Games – in the first four years.

"It's such a great race for runners," says Eleanor Thomas, the first woman to finish in 1975. "It's all about the runners."

As interest in running rose and fell over the next 15 years, participation in the Ottawa Marathon followed suit. The race was almost cancelled in 1986. But fresh leadership and a new, more sustainable running boom soon fuelled a period of growth that exceeded the first wave and the expectations of even the most passionate supporters of the event.

Over the years, the course has been modified, and innovations like electronic timing have been adopted. The event was expanded to include a 10k race on Saturday night, then a half-marathon and 5k race. At the turn of the 21st century, with the support of new sponsors, race officials increased

1983

their efforts to attract elite runners, leading to international attention and new course records. But at the heart of the race have always been the amateur athletes.

Over 39 years, almost 100,000 have followed Jaouhar, Thomas and the other twelve dozen athletes from 1975 to the finish line. Some have done it once, others have finished 30 times or more. Some have crossed in under three hours, others have run or walked for twice as long. Many have used the marathon as a milestone, proof that they have overcome illness, injury, or addiction. Others have raised millions of dollars for important causes like cancer research.

From its modest beginnings four decades ago, the Ottawa Marathon is now clearly established as one of the most popular annual events in the city, and one of the largest and most successful races in North America. More than 7,000 people have registered for the 2014 Ottawa Marathon, and the entire weekend is approaching 50,000 participants.

But much more than one day or one weekend, the marathon has become the focal point for thousands of people – in Ottawa and elsewhere – for the first five months of every year. Starting in January, runners can be seen training all over the city, doing the preparation that will produce results on race day in May.

What brings so many to the start line in Ottawa is not just the enduring appeal of the marathon, but a spectacular course, a meticulously well-organized race, a city that supports running and embraces the event, and a unique opportunity to race alongside thousands of others who share their passion.

It is not just any race. It is Canada's Magnificent Marathon.

2008

1980

2009

1:30
Walking Room
2:15
Running Room
Walking Room
TOLL FREE NUMBER: 1-800-419-2906
5:00
Running Room

1979

1975

146
marathon participants

🌡+15c

2:26:39
Mehdi Jaouhar
Men's Winner

3:27:28
Eleanor Thomas
Women's Winner

The starting line

Many things to do with running and the Ottawa Marathon have changed since the first edition of the race on May 25, 1975.

Training methods have been scientifically refined. Race technology has evolved dramatically; there are no longer volunteers with clipboards to record finishing times. The Ottawa course has been modified several times, and the start and finish areas have moved downtown from Carleton University.

The runners' shoes and clothes are different. And that's not the only way the appearance of marathon participants has changed. Unlike photos from more recent editions, the pictures from the first race show a lot of long hair, mustaches, and not much gender or ethnic diversity.

But one thing that hasn't changed since 1975 is the participation of three men. Every May for 39 years, Howard Cohen, John Stoddart, and Bill Williams have completed the Ottawa Marathon.

Williams was a member of the group that founded the race. Cohen was talked into entering by one of the other founders, Dr. Don Johnson of the sports medicine clinic at Carleton. Stoddart says he saw an article in the *Citizen* and signed up.

"I decided to train for it, not knowing anything about training," he says. "In 1975 there wasn't a lot of information out there. So I ran hard every time."

It was warm on the morning of May 25, 1975. Stoddart remembers Johnson jokingly advising runners to jump in the Rideau Canal if they found the heat getting to them.

"I hit the wall at about 15 miles," says Stoddart. "After that I was walking and running and saying, 'Why the hell am I doing this? This is no fun. I'm never doing this again.'

"And then as soon as it was over I thought, 'When is the next one?'"

Cohen says he and a few other runners felt so depleted they took advantage of an unfortunate ice cream vendor on the side of the course.

"There was a group of about four or five of us who were totally dehydrated," he says. "We spotted an ice cream truck. And the guy got raided. We picked him over. We helped ourselves to a few ice cream bars and we kept on motoring.

"That was the extent of our fluids down the steamy canal. I'm sure the guy never came near the marathon again."

Despite the conditions and making "every beginner mistake that could be made," Cohen says the first race "was enough to hook me."

"I actually enjoyed it even though I fell apart," he says.

Cohen says if he ever stopped running the marathon he would miss the training as much as the race itself.

"I wouldn't trade the training for anything," he says. "Seeing the sun rise – I would miss that more than the marathon. You could give me a million bucks and I'd say keep the million bucks, I'll take the marathon any day."

Along with finishing Ottawa 39 times, Williams has completed about 80 other marathons. He says running helped him deal with his abundance of physical energy and a career spent mostly at a desk.

"It's very hard to give up," he says. "If you stop doing it, you really miss it."

All three men play down the significance of the streak. But none of them has shown any willingness to give it up, not even when they've been injured and almost incapable of running.

"For me, there's never been a thought not to run it," says Williams. "It's just there every year, and you do it."

In 1994, Cohen suffered a torn hamstring while skiing. As a family physician, he says he would have advised a patient under similar circumstances against entering the race. But he went ahead and finished.

In 2010, Stoddart had a painful sciatic nerve. He used crutches for about a quarter of the race, but finished.

All three marvel at how much the event has grown over the past four decades, something neither they nor the other 143 runners could have imagined in 1975.

"I've seen a lot of different changes and, nearly all of it for the better," says Stoddart.

"The event itself has always been magnificent," says Cohen. "It's really a wonderful weekend. It's a weekend to rejoice. I think it's just a wonderful, wonderful event."

"For me, there's never been a thought not to run it. It's just there every year, and you do it. "

BILL WILLIAMS (CENTRE, WITH JOHN STODDART AND HOWARD COHEN)

THE FIRST WOMAN

Of the 146 runners who finished the Ottawa Marathon, only three were women. Although she didn't consider herself the winner, **Eleanor Thomas** was the first of them to finish. See her story in 1976.

FALL OF SAIGON

On April 30, 1975, the Vietnam War ended after American civilians and military personnel were evacuated from Saigon by helicopter.

A NEW STANDARD

Toronto's CN Tower was completed, becoming the world's tallest free-standing structure.

SUMMER BLOCKBUSTER

Directed by Steven Spielberg, *Jaws* opened June 20, 1975 and caused an instant increase in the number of people afraid of swimming in open water.

READY BUT UNPREPARED

Garry Bowes says he and most of the other runners had no idea what to expect from the marathon. "Training was an unknown quantity, and I was totally unaware of the need for distance runs building up to the marathon or for any dietary considerations," he says. Bowes ran five miles a day and threw in an eight-mile and 13-mile run in preparation for the race. "Proper footwear was just becoming available. I had been running in a shoe called a Northstar and developed stress fractures. Adidas produced the SL72 and my feet thanked them. Chafing of clothing wasn't even considered, nor was proper hydration."

Bowes remembers the bibs being made of cloth, and t-shirts that were greenish blue. "When the gun went off, the small knot of runners quickly spread out, and those of us who were mediocre runners soon were alone in an individual race with ourselves."

At the halfway point, Bowes was about to run farther than he ever had before. "Needless to say, as I negotiated the turnaround, I knew real trouble lay ahead! I did begin to reel in runners whose training was perhaps even inferior to mine, but as I headed up the canal towards Carleton my legs tried to resign, and the run in was painful to say the least. Looking back, my 3:56 finish seems rather incredible."

ONLY THE LONELY

Sixteen-year-old **Steve Hambling** finished 16th overall in his first and only marathon. "With such a small field, you were pretty much on your own very quickly into the race, so it truly was the epitome of the loneliness of the long-distance runner," says Hambling. "I think I just kept my pace and didn't stop. My legs got heavy in the last two miles, but I just kept on to the finish with no idea of my placing. The finish line was glorious, with an incredible number of cheering well-wishers waiting for us. We had now returned to the start, Carleton University, so I think I went right into the Carleton Sports Med Clinic and hopped in an ice bath. It was wonderful."

1975

National Capital Marathon

This is to certify that

STEVEN D. HAMBLING

finished 16TH in 2:53:15.0 in the 1st National Capital Marathon

MAY 25, 1975
DATE

JIM McKINNON, Race Director

ACCIDENTAL WINNER

Mehdi Jaouhar, a middle-distance runner from Hull, won the inaugural Ottawa Marathon even though he says he ran the race "by accident." Jaouhar was convinced by his University of Ottawa roommate, Rich Pyne, to enter. The plan was for the two students to run together. "As promised, we ran side-by-side and talking to each other, but at 18 miles, my friend started feeling pain on his left side," Jaouhar remembers. "I waited for him and tried to help him to keep the same pace, but I felt the more I waited, the slower he got. So I told him to keep trying hard and that I must pick up the pace, and I came to the finish line without my best friend." Pyne finished second, two minutes behind the man he had talked into running. Jaouhar never ran another marathon. Now, he says, he runs with his friends for fun, but "of course we fight till the end (to see) who will come first."

BOSTON HERO

Wearing a homemade t-shirt, **Bill Rodgers** was the first to cross the finish line at the Boston Marathon. His time of 2:09:55 broke the course record and was the fastest ever by an American. Rodgers went on to win Boston three more times.

'70S FASHION

Rainbow toe socks were all the rage.

1976

500
marathon participants

🌡+13c

2:16:32
Wayne Yetman
Men's Winner

3:09:27
Eleanor Thomas
Women's Winner

The trailblazer

When she reached the finish line of the 1976 Ottawa Marathon, Eleanor Thomas was greeted by a very enthusiastic friend. That year, Ottawa was the qualification event for the Montreal Olympics, and Thomas was the first woman to cross the finish line.

"So a friend of mine was jumping up and down saying, 'Eleanor is going to the Olympics!'" says Thomas.

Of course, it wasn't until 1984 that women were allowed to run the Olympic marathon. So only the fastest men in Ottawa went on to Montreal in 1976.

In fact, while Thomas was also the first woman to finish in the inaugural Ottawa Marathon in 1975, she received no honour as the top female in either year. There were only overall results, not men's and women's races.

"I wasn't even thinking of winning," she says. "I was just another finisher."

But she wasn't simply any runner to some of the participants. This was only a few years after Kathrine Switzer had forced her way into the Boston Marathon, and many men were still adjusting to running marathons alongside women.

"In those days, there were men who didn't want a woman to finish in front of them," she says "They'd get into races with me. It was really quite hilarious at times."

In 1976, Thomas says, a man tried to block her by passing her and then slowing down in front of her.

"Women just weren't expected to do the things that they're expected to do now," she says. But as more women entered marathons in the years ahead, Thomas says, "The men got over that."

Thomas had no intention of entering marathons when she started running. Her first goal was to quit smoking.

"That was a hopeless task," she says. "I failed and failed. I decided instead of trying to quit something, I should try to do something."

So she took up running with her husband. They soon joined a group of other runners and began training for races in Ottawa and beyond.

"Those were really amazing times to be running in Ottawa," she says. "There was a running boom happening then."

When the group heard about the first Ottawa Marathon being planned for May 1975, they decided to see if they could run that far by attempting one in Montreal in March.

"We thought, if there's going to be a marathon let's see if we can run that far," she says. "We just trained and did it. Nobody had a clue what training actually was. We'll just go down and see if we can actually do it. And we did."

Thomas became very involved in the Ottawa running community, helping to launch the National Capital Runners Association, eventually becoming president and also producing the organization's monthly newsletter on a manual typewriter.

"There were terrific people involved," she says. "The running community was so great back then. So supportive and encouraging of each other."

Thomas went on to run a total of 14 or 15 marathons, including a personal best of three hours and two minutes. After a long break from racing, she entered Ottawa in 2009, when the event fell on her 65th birthday.

"I thought, this is a sign," she said. But one month before the race, she was hit by a bicycle on one of her training runs and broke her arm. She ran the race with a cast and finished in just over five hours.

"The volunteers were still there and they were still enthused," she says. "It was as if I was the winner. The greatest thing about the race is the volunteers."

Thomas says she wanted her last marathon to be under five hours, so she entered again in 2010 and finished in 4:52.

"I managed to be under five hours," she says. "I thought, that's the end of my marathon career."

Nevertheless, she continues to run 40 to 50 kilometres a week for fitness. And even if she was never given a gold medal or prize money, Eleanor Thomas will always be the first woman ever to finish the Ottawa Marathon.

"I wasn't even thinking of winning ...I was just another finisher."

ELEANOR THOMAS

FIRST OF MANY

Future Canadian Road Running Hall of Fame inductee **Diane Palmason** finished her first marathon in 3:54. With her twelve-year-old son Craig cycling beside her and wearing a watch, Palmason methodically ran a nine-minute mile pace. In some cases, if she hit the mile mark too fast, she stopped and walked until nine minutes were up. Palmason went on to run 78 marathons (see her story in 1985).

ONE FOR THE AGES

A new Canadian marathon record for 45-year-old men was set by **Arthur Taylor**. His time of 2:26:35 still stands and is one of the oldest Canadian masters road records.

ONE OF A HANDFUL

Running her first Ottawa Marathon, Ottawa's **Cheryl Kardish-Levitan** was the third woman to finish. "It sounds impressive but there were probably a handful of women," she says. She has since run 27 marathons (see her story in 2005).

FATHER AND SON

Legendary marathoner **Ed Whitlock**, who went on to set multiple age-group records in his seventies and eighties, ran the marathon with his 15-year-old son Clive, winning the father-son competition in a time of 2:52:00.

THE NATION'S BEST

With the Montreal Games just weeks away, the Ottawa Marathon was chosen as the site of the Olympic trials, attracting many of Canada's top marathoners.

1976

CANADA HOSTS THE WORLD

For the first time ever, Canada played host to the Olympics. Under tight security and running 'way over budget, the Games were held in Montréal. Waldemar Cierpinski of East Germany won the marathon (there was no women's event). Romanian gymnast Nadia Comaneci won three gold medals and became the first to be awarded a perfect score of 10 in an Olympic gymnastic event.

FLIGHT OF THE CONCORDE

Flight BA300 left London Heathrow for Bahrain on January 21, 1976. The Concorde had to go through 5,000 hours of testing before it was certified for passenger flight. Its fastest transatlantic crossing – from New York to London – took just 2 hours 52 minutes and 59 seconds, less time than it took the top female finisher to complete the 1976 Ottawa marathon.

PLAY BALL!

Toronto was awarded a Major League baseball team.

RUNNING TO THE THEATRE

Dustin Hoffman starred in *The Marathon Man*. The highest grossing film of the year was *Rocky*, which earned $225 million in global box office receipts. The film was made on a budget of just over $1 million and shot in 28 days.

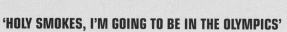

'HOLY SMOKES, I'M GOING TO BE IN THE OLYMPICS'

After breaking away from the lead pack in the 1976 Ottawa Marathon, **Wayne Yetman** says he thought, "Holy smokes, I'm going to be in the Olympics. I better not goof this up." Yetman won a spot in the Montreal Games and relished his Olympic moment, including lunch with the Queen. "There were only eight of us at the table," he says. "That was a thrilling experience for me." A week before the Olympic marathon, Yetman was encouraged by his final long training run. "I ran like I've never run in my life." But by race day he was suffering from a cold and struggled. The disappointment, he says, still haunts him to this day. But the Ottawa race, he says, "led to some wonderful life experiences and running experiences. I'm grateful to Ottawa."

1977

The 87-pound teenager

1,250
marathon participants

+11c

2:18:05
Mike Dyon
Men's Winner

3:02:22
Joann McKinty-Heale
Women's Winner

Sometimes when you take on a big challenge, you're better off not knowing how difficult it will be. In 1977, when a 13-year-old named Adrian "Punky" Baird ran the Ottawa Marathon one week after a gruelling 55-kilometre charity event, he simply didn't know any better.

"I was pretty naïve," says Baird. "But the key thing was nobody told you what you could or couldn't do, or how bad it was going to be.

"Now you plan for the worst. Back then we had no idea."

Baird grew up in Ottawa and says his nickname started when his younger sister couldn't pronounce his given name. To this day, he says, everyone in his family still calls him Punky. The name was a good fit for a kid with a slight frame. Baird says he weighed about 87 pounds when he was 13.

He took up running in school and loved it so much, he ran whenever he had the opportunity. He trained with older teenagers and even runners who were old enough to be his parents.

"I was a bit hyper," says Baird. "I used to run home for lunch because otherwise I couldn't make it there and back in time. I ran at recess. And I ran track."

So when he entered the 1977 Metres for Millions, which was supposed to be a 55-kilometre fundraising walk, he decided rather than take is slowly like everyone else, he would run.

He remembers arriving at water stations along the route and surprising the volunteers who weren't expecting participants to arrive for hours to come. When his run was over, he called home to see if one of his parents could pick him up. But they were hosting a barbecue so he took the bus.

"Most people finished at midnight," he says. "I ran it in about five hours. I took the bus home and delivered my newspapers."

Sometime after the charity event, a friend suggested he do the marathon. Which happened to be the following weekend.

"I said, okay let's do it," he says. "I didn't know about training or tapering."

Baird finished in a fast three hours and 12 minutes, but the race was by no means easy.

"It hurt," he says. "It was all good until about 20 miles. Then I hit the wall. I didn't know what the wall was at that time. I had no idea what was going on."

Another runner put his arm around Baird and coaxed him to continue. He finished the race and this time his father was there to pick him up and take him out for a hamburger.

The following year, Baird ran Ottawa again, and finished in 2:46. He went on to run a 2:42 at another event later that year, which is actually faster than the published record for 14-year-old runners.

"Flaked out", May 15/77 – 3:12:58
NATIONAL CAPITAL MARATHON

Also in 1978, Baird went to watch the Commonwealth Games in Edmonton, where he saw Jerome Drayton win the silver medal for Canada. Drayton went on to win the Ottawa Marathon in 1979 and set the Canadian marathon record, which would stand for decades.

"He was my hero," says Baird. "He was amazing."

After those quick marathons at a young age, Baird took some time off from running, but came back to the sport in his last year of high school, turning in some strong finishes in provincial and national events. But a series of ailments that affected his muscle strength forced him to give it up again.

More recently, Baird has started running for fitness, doing more sensible distances of 14 to 16 kilometres. No monster runs on consecutive weekends.

With the benefit of hindsight, his adventures as a teenage marathoner seem audacious.

"Doing 55k and then running a marathon the next weekend," he says, "That was ridiculous."

"The key thing was nobody told you what you could or couldn't do, or how bad it was going to be."

ADRIAN "PUNKY" BAIRD

"I CAME TO WIN"

It was his first marathon, but 21-year-old **Mike Dyon** told the *Ottawa Citizen*, "I came to win." And he did win, outrunning what was then the largest field ever assembled for a marathon in Canada, 1,250 participants. Dyon went on to capture Ottawa again in 1981 and 1983, becoming the first multiple winner of the race. And just a few days before he won Ottawa for the first time, Dyon became president of Brooks Canada, going on to become a leader in the running community in Canada.

RUNNING IN PAIN

The 1977 race was one **Eleanor Thomas** remembers well, but not because she performed well. The two-time women's winner sustained a serious injury months before the event and says she was not ready for another marathon when May arrived. "I suffered a lot on the day. I ran 3:24:30, well off my best. Much pain. I never completely recovered from that injury, and it was years before I was pain-free."

BOX OFFICE FORCE

Just a few weeks after the Ottawa Marathon, the most lucrative movie franchise in history was launched. Star Wars was released on May 25.

THE KING IS DEAD

On August 16, music legend **Elvis Presley** died at the age of 42.

PREGNANT PAUSE

Dr. James Dickson of Ottawa ran the marathon for the first time, and continued running it for the next eight years. He had planned to run his first Ottawa Marathon in 1976 but at the last minute he was called away to deliver a baby. "I was up all night and in no shape to run the next morning," says Dickson.

ROCK & ROLL SINGER, 1935-1977

29 USA

ELVIS

RECORD-SETTING SEASON

The Montreal Canadiens became the first team in NHL history to win 60 games in a season when they beat the Capitals 2-1 at Washington to finish with a record of 60-8-12. **Jacques Lemaire** (#25) scored the overtime winner to seal the Habs' Cup victory in 1977.

1977

DRAYTON TRIUMPHS IN BOSTON

Canadian runner **Jerome Drayton** won the Boston Marathon in a time of 2:14:46.

NEW YORK, NEW YORK

Bill Rodgers won the New York City Marathon for the second year in a row, in a time of 2:11:28.

1978

Two-tenths of a second

MAY 14

2,600
marathon participants

🌡 **+14c**

2:16:03
Brian Maxwell
Men's Winner

2:47:37
Christine Lavallée
Women's Winner

Before he founded the multi-million-dollar sports nutrition giant PowerBar, Brian Maxwell had another claim to fame: In 1978, he prevailed in what was then the narrowest recorded marathon victory in history, winning by only two-tenths of a second in a thrilling sprint to the finish line in Ottawa.

Maxwell says the Ottawa spectators played a big role in his triumph. Halfway through the race, Maxwell trailed Paul Bannon by a significant margin. He was about to settle for second place – the top two finishers would qualify for the Commonwealth Games in Edmonton that summer – but the spectators encouraged him to chase Bannon down.

"People were yelling, 'Go get him!'" says Ken Parker, the race director that year. "They shamed him into making an effort."

"He said that made him feel kind of guilty being in second place," says Martin Cleary, who covered the 1978 race and about 30 other Ottawa Marathons for the *Ottawa Citizen*. "That got him going, and he caught up with Bannon."

Wearing white shorts adorned with red maple leaves, Maxwell reached Bannon in the final 10 kilometres, and for the rest of the race they battled back and forth for the lead.

Parker says he never expected such a close race. Maxwell was considered one of the top endurance runners in Canada; Bannon was running his first marathon.

"For two guys to go at it over six miles, that's really unusual" he says. "You might get it for a mile sometimes. But that was rare."

"The crowd at the finish was about three or four deep for about 50 or 100 metres," says Cleary. "It was very noisy. Maxwell and Bannon came around the final turn and they went head-to-head in a good old-fashioned sprint to the line."

At the last moment, Maxwell beat Bannon by half a stride. "It was a thrilling finish," says Cleary.

In 1993, Cleary spoke to Maxwell about his memories of that close finish. "To run 42 kilometres and win, basically by a lean, is definitely a thrill," he said.

Parker says race officials were later told it was the smallest margin of victory of any marathon in history.

Maxwell was born in England, but grew up in Toronto. He competed in track-and-field during high school, and earned an athletic scholarship to the University of California at Berkeley.

He wasn't a typical long-distance runner. He was diagnosed with a defective heart valve that cost him some of his aerobic power. And Parker says the first time he met Maxwell, he didn't believe he was an elite marathoner.

"I met him at the airport," he says. "I thought, this guy's kind of short and kind of stocky. Not your normal marathon body."

Yet by 1977, Maxwell was ranked as the third-best marathon runner in the world by Track and Field News. He was a member of Canada's Olympic team in 1980, but never competed because of a boycott.

And in the mid-1980s, he and his future wife Jennifer began experimenting with nutritional solutions for endurance athletes. The result was PowerBar, a pioneering product in what would become a multibillion-dollar market for energy bars and sports supplements.

The Maxwells started making PowerBars in their kitchen. Along with a partner, they built the company into a 300-person enterprise with sales of $150 million. In 2000, they sold it to Nestle for a reported $375 million, much of which they donated to athletic facilities and support for young athletes.

In 2004, at the age of 51, Maxwell suffered a fatal heart attack near his home in California. His life was short but his legacy includes the invention of the energy bar, a long list of philanthropic contributions, and a thrilling come-from-behind victory in the Ottawa Marathon.

"To run 42 kilometres and win, basically by a lean, is definitely a thrill."

BRIAN MAXWELL (RIGHT)

REPEAT AFTER ME
The Simon memory toy hit the market.

WELCOME TO OTTAWA
Inspired by friends, **Patrick Deutscher** of Toronto ran his first marathon, and his first race since grade school. "I was 27 years old, and had been running with friends for fitness for a couple of years," he says. "I had been surprised and intrigued to hear that they ran marathons, so I decided to give it a try. My time was about 3:13, and I was pretty elated, despite quads that were stiff as boards later in the day."

47 COUNTRIES, 1,475 ATHLETES
The Queen officially opened the 11th Commonwealth Games in Edmonton in August.

KEEPSAKE
Jacques Menard still has his t-shirt from the Ottawa Marathon in 1978. He ran Ottawa for the first time in 1976 as a 15-year-old. "I often joke that I may hold the record for the 15-and-younger age group, knowing that 15-year-olds can no longer run a marathon," says Menard. "I was very nervous at the time, but was also very much encouraged by the older runners."

FUTURE OLYMPIAN
Wearing bib number 1590, **Ellen Rochefort** of Aylmer, Quebec ran the second-fastest marathon by a Canadian woman, finishing the race in 2:52:24. Rochefort went on to compete for Canada at the 1988 Olympic Games in Seoul, coming in 31st in the marathon with a time of 2:36:44.

DOUBLE MEDALS
The 1978 Ottawa Marathon was the men's qualifier for the Commonwealth Games in Edmonton that summer. **Jerome Drayton** was exempt from having to run the trials based on his victories at the 1976 Fukuoka Marathon in Japan and the Boston Marathon in 1977. Drayton won the silver medal at the Games. Fellow Canadian Paul Bannon won the bronze.

THE NEW BISHOP OF ROME

Karol Józef Wojtyła succeeded John Paul I to become Pope John Paul II. He was the first non-Italian pontiff since the 16th century, and the first Polish and Slavic pope.

1978

STRONG FIELD

A fast group of runners battled it out for a chance to represent Canada at the Commonwealth Games in Edmonton. Some of the leaders shown early in the race include **Nil Lavallee**, **Mike Dyon**, **Brian Maxwell**, **Dave Northey**, **Paul Bannon**, **Brian Armstrong**, **Wayne Yetman** and **Don Howieson**.

LEGEND IN THE MAKING

Jacqueline Gareau ran the Ottawa Marathon for the first time in 3:07:19. See her story in 1979.

FLYING HIGH

Runners from The RAF's marathon team travelled from Britain to compete in the Ottawa Marathon. Pictured are **Doug Couie**, **Nick Rust**, **Andy Law**, **Bob King**, **Alextair Watt**, **Paul Wright** and **Dave Todd**.

NO PUNCH BACKS

After nearly 30 years, production of the Volkswagen Beetle is stopped.

1979

"I loved to run long"

2,932
marathon participants

🌡+15c

2:18:05
Jerome Drayton
Men's Winner

2:47:58
Jacqueline Gareau
Women's Winner

She was named the top Canadian marathoner of the 20th century. She won the Ottawa Marathon in 1979. And she prevailed in one of the most famous Boston Marathons of all time. But Jacqueline Gareau started entering long-distance races not because she wanted to compete, but simply because she loved to run.

"I was running with friends, doing three hours and feeling fresh," she says. "I was running just because I loved to run long. And someone said, 'Why don't you run a marathon?'"

That was in 1977, not long after Gareau had taken up the sport and just three years before she won Boston in historic fashion. Gareau had been working as a respiratory technician in a Montreal hospital in the mid-1970s when a colleague suggested she join him for a run.

"I saw all these people smoking and getting sick and dying with a cigarette in their mouths," she says. "I decided to stop smoking. And he said, 'Why don't we go for a jog?'

"I went for a 20-minute run and I barely stopped. After that I just kept running."

Within a few months, she was regularly ascending Mont Royal as part of hour-long runs and thinking, "Wow, I feel so good," she says.

"I just kept running because running felt good to me," she says. "I loved running long distances."

In her first marathon in 1977, she finished in three hours and 44 minutes. That's a respectable time, but it didn't foreshadow a career as a champion. Gareau, though, was determined to improve with each race. And within a few marathons, she had established herself as one of the fastest long-distance runners in Canada.

"It was fun," she says. "I wasn't checking much who else was there and who should I keep an eye

> **"I don't want to do it too much. But I end up every season doing too much because it's hard to stop."**

on. I was just doing it to do the best I could do. That was my target."

She finished second in Ottawa in 1978, in three hours and seven minutes. The next year, she won the race in just under two hours and 48 minutes.

"Ottawa was the best race in Canada," she says. "Everyone from Montreal wanted to do it."

Gareau planned to run Ottawa again in 1980, but a friend suggested she run Boston instead. That friend ended up becoming her husband.

"I think he had his eye on me at the time," she says.

It was a historic decision. In Boston, Gareau won one of the most controversial and infamous marathons in history. She was declared the winner three days after the race when it was discovered that the first woman across the finish line had not run the entire course.

The woman who cheated denied Gareau the thrill of breaking the tape as the winner, but the astonishing turn of events gave her a special place in running lore. She is regularly welcomed back to Boston for special anniversaries and ceremonies.

Gareau went on win seven other marathons, and represented Canada at the Olympics in 1984. She also captured the gruelling Mount Washington Road Race three times.

She still runs regularly and still enjoys long distances, but runs marathons only occasionally, saying she likes to save her strength for the physical demands of her job as a massage therapist.

"I enter races because I like the people," she says. "I don't want to do it too much. But I end up every season doing too much because it's hard to stop."

As for her 1979 win in Ottawa, one of the breakthrough performances on the way to a legendary career, she says, "I have very good memories of the Ottawa Marathon. It's a great course and it's very well-organized."

SOLO DAD

Running without either of his sons for the first time in Ottawa, **Ed Whitlock** finished in a time of 2:31, a personal best.

DEBATING WHETHER TO RUN

David Johnston, the future Governor General of Canada, was registered to run his first marathon in Ottawa with a friend. But a month before the race, Johnston was asked to moderate the federal leaders' debate between Ed Broadbent, Joe Clark and Pierre Trudeau. "Then I realized that the debate was on the Sunday night and we were to run the marathon on the Sunday (morning)," says Johnston. The debate was in Ottawa, and at first Johnston thought he could still do both events. But he reconsidered at the last minute, deciding that if he made a mistake during the debate, people would blame it on the fact that he'd run a marathon that morning. His only regret was letting down his friend. "And I felt so badly about it that we determined that we'd do it the next year, and we did," he says.

Husband, Wife Finish Marathon

OTTAWA — Mike and Nancy Mieszczak of Buffalo were husband-and-wife marathon finishers in the National Capitol Marathon held here Sunday.

Mike ran the 26-mile, 385-yard race in 2 hours, 45 minutes, 19 seconds and Nancy ran in 2:55, the third woman finisher. Also competing from Buffalo were Paul McDonnell, 2:54; John Annoni, 3:08; Bruce Kovach, 3:09; Wayne Steepus, 3:12; Bob Ivory, 3:22; Jerry Soloman, 3:28 and Dale Eddolls, 3:47.

The race was won by Jerome Drayton of Toronto in 2:17. Jacqueline Gareau won the women's competition in 2:47.

A CUP FOR THE COUPLE

Mike and Nancy Meiszezk of Buffalo both ran the marathon. Mike finished in 2:45:19, and Nancy finished third in the women's division in a time of 2:55. They received special mugs as the top finishing couple. The Meiszezks were part of a group of Buffalo runners, which also include **Paul McDonnell** (shown above), taking part in the Ottawa Marathon that year.

PORTABLE, SORT OF

Sony introduced the Walkman TPS-L2 – a 14-ounce, blue-and-silver portable cassette player with a leather case, chunky buttons, headphones, and a second earphone jack so two people could listen in at once. On her blog, marathoner **Lynn Kobayashi** (see her story in 1983) remembers what running with the first "personal music device" was like. "The prototype was a behemoth," she wrote, "and to run with it involved a complicated system of belts and strapping which felt like being wrapped in a very wide tensor bandage."

1979

THE IRON LADY ARRIVES

Winning the May election, **Margaret Thatcher** became the first woman to be prime minister of the United Kingdom.

A BORING WIN

In his only appearance at the Ottawa Marathon, legendary Canadian runner **Jerome Drayton** won by such a wide margin that he described the race as "boring." Race officials had hoped to use Drayton's appearance to promote the event, but he refused to commit until the last minute. "He told us, 'It depends on the weather,'" says former race organizer Ken Parker. "He said, 'If it looks good, I may drive up Saturday.'" Drayton could be aloof and even, according to 1976 champion Wayne Yetman, crude. "He was an interesting character," says Yetman. "You'd certainly get entertained on a run with him." But Yetman says, "He was a beautiful runner to watch." Drayton's time of 2:10:08 at the Fukuoka Marathon in 1975 is still the fastest ever run by a Canadian, and in 1977 he became the first and still the only Canadian man to win the Boston Marathon since 1948.

42 IS THE ANSWER

The Hitchhiker's Guide to the Galaxy by Douglas Adams was published. If 42 is the answer to everything in the universe, that includes the number of kilometres in a marathon.

SHOE NEWS

Nike launched Nike Air technology in the Tailwind running shoe.

1980

4,388
marathon participants

🌡+12c

2:22:54
Patrick Montuoro
Men's Winner

2:42:50
Christine Lavallée
Women's Winner

The start of something special

At a turnaround in the 1980 Ottawa Marathon, Lou Mulvihill remembers seeing the faces of runners who noticed him for the first time.

"I could see the people on the other side of the road," he says. "It was probably the first time they saw somebody in a wheelchair attempt something like that.

"They actually started clapping when I went by. I thought, 'Wow.' I actually got a lump in my throat."

The previous year, Mulvihill became the first person to complete the Ottawa Marathon in a wheelchair. In 1980, he was joined by four other athletes with disabilities. At the time, there was no separate category for wheelchair athletes, so they raced alongside runners, many of whom were surprised and inspired by what they saw.

"I opened the eyes of a lot of runners," he says. "That was back in the day when if you were disabled, you couldn't do much. I guess I opened my own eyes too."

Nine years earlier, a motorcycle accident had left Mulvihill with only partial use of his legs. In the first few days, he didn't accept the extent to which his life had changed.

"My father was a doctor," he says, "I was under the impression that he could just fix me up and get me back on my feet and get me going again."

After competing in track and cross-country in high school, Mulvihill was faced with the news that he wouldn't be able to run anymore. He decided, "I'm still going to live a long life and make the most of it."

So he began competing in wheelchair basketball and track, and eventually longer races.

"I knew I had endurance, I knew I had the drive," he says. "If I built the right chair, I knew I could do the marathon."

Racing wheelchairs were even more primitive than running shoes in those days. So using bicycle parts, Mulvihill fashioned a three-wheel racing chair. He got as much enjoyment from building his own equipment as he did from training.

Once he had designed a proper racing chair, he entered the Ottawa Marathon.

"I just registered like everybody else," he says.

Today, wheelchair athletes typically start before the rest of the field, and many of them travel much faster than the average runner. But at the start of his first marathon, Mulvihill was worried about getting in the way.

"I didn't want anyone to trip over me," he says, "so I started off to the side."

It turns out he had nothing to worry about. The other athletes were nothing but welcoming to him.

"There was no negative reaction at all. It was all positive," he says. "It was a little bit overwhelming. I'm sure I probably gave them the impression that if that guy can do it in the wheelchair, *I* better finish the race."

Mulvihill hopes that in his two Ottawa Marathons, he helped to change attitudes about people with disabilities.

"I wanted the public to get used to and be comfortable with wheelchairs in society," he says. "Now it's almost matter-of-fact when you see someone in a wheelchair. It wasn't then."

When he crossed the finish line, Mulvihill says he felt relieved and excited.

"I accomplished something that I thought was pretty darn good," he says. "I thought, if you can do that, you can do anything."

Indeed, it was just the beginning. Mulvihill went on to become a successful sledge-hockey player, playing on three World-Cup-winning teams and serving as captain of Team Canada.

"But it all started with the marathon," he says. "That was my first big accomplishment."

"There was no negative reaction at all. It was all positive."

LOU MULVIHILL

NEVER TOO OLD

The oldest man to run the 1980 Ottawa Marathon was 69-year-old Dave Kaufman of North Bay, Ontario. The oldest woman was Judith Kazdan, 60, of Willowdale, Ontario.

NEVER TOO YOUNG

Alan Forster ran his second Ottawa marathon – and fourth marathon overall — at the age of 10. Alan was the youngest entrant in 1980 – but there were 14 boys and three girls age 14 and under who ran that year. He ran much of the marathon with his father John, but at mile 19 set off on his own because his dad "couldn't keep up." He went on win a national cross-country title while at the University of Ottawa. He is now Dr. Alan Forster and continues to run.

MAGIC

The 3-D combination puzzle *Rubik's Cube* – originally called the Magic Cube – was licensed by Rubik to be sold by Ideal Toy Corp.

INTERNATIONAL FIELD

The field in 1989 had two runners from New Zealand, two Germans, one from Australia, one from the Netherlands, and 343 from the United States.

RECOVERY

Marathoner **Larry Scarborough** took a much-deserved rest in the medical tent after finishing the race.

THE CANADIAN CAPER
Ken Taylor, Canadian ambassador to Iran, became an international celebrity for helping six Americans escape Tehran in what was called the Canadian Caper.

1980

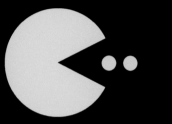

CHOMP
The classic video game Pac-Man was released, eventually becoming a pop-culture icon of the 1980s.

IT'S OFFICIAL
O Canada is adopted as Canada's national anthem.

TOP AMERICAN
Kare Cossaboon, of New York State, was the top American finisher in a time of 2:55:31. It was the first marathon in which she broke three hours. "She has run 35 marathons in her career and says Ottawa was "one of the most beautiful marathons" she ever ran. Cossaboon remembers spectators yelling in French, which she didn't understand, and throwing candies at the runners. She went on to be a U.S. Olympic Marathon Trials qualifier in 1984 and 1988. At that time, she and her husband **Craig Holm** were the fastest road-racing couple in the United States, holding the record for a combined marathon time.

MARATHON OF HOPE
Terry Fox started his Marathon of Hope on April 12, 1980, dipping his artificial leg into the Atlantic Ocean off the coast of St John's, Newfoundland. For 143 days Fox ran an average of a marathon a day to raise money for cancer research. But after 5,373 kilometres, Fox was forced to stop his run outside of Thunder Bay, Ontario after his cancer spread to his lungs. When he died the following year, he had met his goal of raising one dollar for every Canadian. But that was just the beginning. The Terry Fox Foundation has since raised more than $600 million.

RUNNING, NOT TIPTOEING
Christine Lavallee, who was the top woman in 1978, won Ottawa again with a time of 2:47:37. In a 1984 *Ottawa Citizen* article, Lavallee said the Ottawa race always makes her think of tulips. "They made it really refreshing, even for a marathon."

1981

Going out on top

Just seconds after crossing the finish line in Ottawa in 1981, Ken Parker made a very big decision. He would never run another marathon.

Some runners promise themselves "never again" after a gruelling marathon. But Parker's vow didn't arise from pain or disappointment; it was because the race had gone exceptionally well.

Parker was one of the runners who launched the Ottawa Marathon in 1975, and, despite having many responsibilities as one of the main organizers of the event each year, he ran the first seven editions of the race.

"I'd be running around frantically until about ten minutes before the race, then I'd go strip off my sweats and warm up for a couple of minutes and wait for the gun," he says. "Then, once I was finished running, I went back to work on the event."

In 1981, something special happened. After 13 years of running marathons and always finishing with a feeling that he could go still faster, Parker posted his best time ever: two hours and 42 minutes.

"My training had been perfect," he says. "I knew that I was the fittest I had ever been. And the weather was perfect. It was cool with just a spit of rain. The planets were aligned. It was meant to be."

Parker says he made the decision quickly because he knew those factors would never come together again on the same day.

"That's why I was able to say, 'This is it, I'm drawing a line under it,'" he says. "I didn't want to run slower times. It was always about challenging myself and getting faster. So there was no point in going on, because I couldn't possibly run any faster."

None of Parker's friends believed him when he said he was retiring from the marathon. "People said, 'You say this after every marathon,'" he says. "Which was true."

And the following year, when Parker was standing at the start line with legendary CFRA broadcaster Ernie Calcutt, he briefly had second thoughts.

"It was a sunny day and we were watching the excitement of people getting ready for the race," says Parker. "Ernie said to me, 'Every year you've run this race. Do you wish you were out there?' And I said, 'I thought I was okay, but now I'm starting to wonder if I shouldn't be out there.'"

But once the race started, any regrets soon disappeared. And Parker says that was the only time he had any second thoughts about his decision.

"Other than that, I've never had any hesitation that I made the right decision," he says.

Parker jokes that while his time was quick, it wasn't even the fastest in his neighbourhood. In the days when the marathon was less-popular, those who did enter the race were generally quite fast.

"I ran a 2:42 and I wasn't even the fastest guy on my street," he says. "There was a Masters runner who was faster and there was a kid I was coaching who was faster."

Parker didn't run another marathon, but he continued to play a leadership role in the Ottawa event for another five years, helping to sustain the race through some challenging times. But when he thinks back on those years, the memory that stands out above all others is his personal best time.

"I set out to do something and committed to do it in my training, and to make it all happen was extremely satisfying," he says. "I felt euphoric, and not sad at all to be retiring from marathons. For me it was mission accomplished.

"It was like retiring after winning the gold medal. That was my gold medal."

"I knew that I was the fittest I had ever been. And the weather was perfect. The planets were aligned. It was meant to be."

KEN PARKER

A HELPING HAND
The Canadarm is first used on the Space Shuttle Columbia.

HAND-IN-HAND
Running partners **Jay Thomson** and **Robert Brown** of Waterloo crossed the line in 27th and 28th place, holding hands. "While we trained together for years and pushed one another, we always raced as individuals. That day neither could best the other," says Thomson. "Rob always got me on shorter distances. He had jumped me just at the line in another Ottawa, a fact he never has let me forget!"

WINNERS AND CO-WORKERS
Kathryn Tanner won the Ottawa Marathon in a time of 2:48:54. She went on to become the promotions and advertising director of Brooks Canada – the company run by this year's men's champion, **Mike Dyon**.

CARRY ME HOME
Marathoner **Guy Des Biens** collapsed at the finish line, but was supported by another runner.

ASSASSINATION ATTEMPT
Ronald Reagan, press secretary James Brady, Washington police officer Thomas Delahanty, and Secret Service agent Timothy McCarthy were struck by gunfire from would-be assassin John Hinckley, Jr. outside the Washington Hilton Hotel on March 30.

STICKY SITUATION
Post-it notes were launched by 3M in Canada and Europe.

FAST GROUP
A total of 630 of the 3,478 finishers completed the course in under three hours.

CHERISHED MOMENT
Toward the end of his third Ottawa Marathon, **René Cournoyer** was surprised by his daughter Eve, who joined him for the final minutes the race. It is a moment – and a photo – he still cherishes. Eve Cournoyer became a well-known signer-songwriter in Quebec before she passed away in 2012.

Dad, kids try big run

GO, GIRLS
Raymond Metcalfe of Deep River, Ontario may have started out training for the Ottawa marathon alone, but he soon had some company. Raymond's three daughters, **Abbigail**, **Ailsa**, and **Yvette** (9, 11, and 13) all end up running the marathon as well. The youngest of the three girls, Abbigail, didn't want to be left out, so she trained after school every day with her older sisters. Raymond says he didn't push them, but allowed them to run on the condition that they work up to a 20-mile training run by one week before the marathon. And they did it. All three are now active women, still running, cycling, and doing other sports.

JOLLY GOOD START
Thousands of people ran through the normally quiet Sunday morning streets of the British capital in the first ever London Marathon.

IDENTICAL RESULTS
Identical twin sisters **Sylvaine** and **Patricia Puntous** of Montreal placed second and third, crossing the finish line almost simultaneously in 2:48:59. They went on to be two of the best triathletes in Canada, winning first and second at the Hawaii Ironman in 1983 and 1984.

LEAVING IT OUT THERE
Dennis Bowles was supported by race volunteers after he collapses at the finish line.

1982

The longest hundred metres

Paul Bush covered the first 42.1 kilometres of the 1982 Ottawa Marathon in less than three hours. But it took him six weeks to complete the last 100 metres.

After training in the cold Ottawa winter, Bush struggled with the heat and humidity on race day, and collapsed in the final stretch at Carleton University, with the finish line in sight.

"I was completely dehydrated and overheated," he says. "My core temperature was right off the charts."

According to Bush, his wife Sue speculated that the top woman in the race was approaching, and he didn't want to finish behind her.

"That's my wife's version," he says. "That's not necessarily my version. I guess in the end, the top female stepped over me."

Bush says he was a pretty good cross-country runner in high school, but had never considered doing a marathon. "My wife forced me to do it, so I did," he says.

In 1981, before they were married, they trained together, and Bush ran his first marathon in Ottawa, in cooler conditions. He finished in an impressive time of two hours and 49 minutes.

The following January, Paul and Sue were married, and began training to run Ottawa again. Through the first 35 kilometres on race day, Bush says he felt good. But he doesn't remember much after passing Parliament Hill and heading south on Colonel By Drive with about five kilometres to go.

Bush's brother-in-law, who was following him on a bicycle, says he started struggling and was having difficulty maintaining a straight line, sometimes drifting off course and bumping into the curb. But he kept going and reached the final few hundred metres of the race.

"I guess I could see the finish line," says Bush.

"It was about a hundred metres to go. I probably picked it up a bit. Whatever the reason, I fell down, got up, fell down again, and didn't get up."

Medical volunteers rushed to Bush's side and began to ice his overheated body. Within minutes, they were rushing him to hospital.

While he was being treated, race officials waited for Sue to complete her race.

"She gets to the finish line and there's a big entourage there and she figures she's won something," says Bush. "No, it's that your husband's in the hospital."

Bush says he woke up six or seven hours later with tubes coming out of his body. He thought he had been in a car accident.

"They were flushing me with fluids," he says. "Trying to get my core temperature down. They were monitoring my internal organs to make sure they came back to normal."

The dehydration was severe, and Bush ended up spending a week recovering in hospital.

A few weeks after he was discharged, race organizers offered him a chance to pick up where he had left off.

"They set up the finish line again and let me start from the prone position and run the last hundred metres. I got down on the ground, got up and finished the thing.

"I forget what the headline was, but it was something like, "Six Weeks, Three Days, and 22 Hours Later, He Finally Finishes the Marathon."

Bush never attempted to run 42.2 kilometres again. "After that, my wife and mother didn't want me to run any others," he says. "So I concentrated on 10k races and cross-country runs.

"That was my last marathon."

It took a long time to complete, but it left Bush with a great story to tell.

Recovered runner back on track

By Tony Lofaro
Citizen staff writer

On a cool and wet Friday morning, Paul Bush finally completed the race that had almost cost him his life.

In a ceremonial finishing run yesterday at Carleton University, marathon organizers allowed Bush to complete the final 200 metres of the race.

and 15 seconds per mile that I had set for myself."

Bush, an administrative supervisor at Telesat Canada, said he realized he wasn't drink-

> " **I forget what the headline was, but it was something like, "Six Weeks, Three Days, and 22 Hours Later, He Finally Finishes the Marathon."** "

PAUL BUSH

PASSING LANE

Wearing bib 105, **Muya Wachira**, (shown here with **Matthew Grasmeyer** and **John Clarke**), was the top local finisher in a time of 2:30:23. In the last 11 kilometres of the race, Wachira picked up the pace to pass nine runners and come in in fifth place.

RACING TO THE FINISH IN BOSTON

Alberto Salazar and **Dick Beardsley** became the first two runners to break 2:09:00 in the same race after dueling one another for first place over the final nine miles of the Boston Marathon.

PERSONAL BEST

Lynn Kobayashi of Toronto finished her second marathon in a time of 3:37 – more than a half-hour faster than her first marathon the year before.

SPANNING THE AGES

The youngest person to run the race in 1982 was nine-year-old Jeffrey Cloutier of Ottawa. Claire Beland, age 10, was the youngest female, while the oldest female was 61-year-old Fu-Yung Chou of Toronto. George Capraru of Toronto and Ottawa **Egons Rupners** were the oldest runners, at 70.

YOUR CHARIOT AWAITS

Brooks introduced its famous Chariot shoe – a revolutionary shoe featuring Diagonal "Rollbar" technology.

HOLDING A 20-YEAR RECORD

Peterborough's **Rayma Dixon** took up running in 1973 at the age of 42 and has run marathons all over North America. In 1982, she got three records at the Masters' North American Track and Field Championships in Ottawa. She also established the Canadian marathon record for women over age 50 that year at the National Capital Marathon, finishing in 3:15:50 – a record that stood for 20 years, until it was beaten by Louise Voghel of Saint-Armand, Quebec in November 2004.

AMERICANS ON TOP

For the first time, American runners took both top spots at the Ottawa Marathon. **Greg Leroy** of Oklahoma and **Margo Elson** of California were the winners. It was the third time Leroy had run the Ottawa marathon – he finished second in the previous two years. In 1982, he won by more than five minutes. The women's race was expected to be a tight battle between the previous year's winner, Kathryn Tanner of Toronto, and Elson, but Tanner ended up dropping out of the race at the 8 km mark because of a back seizure. "It was a tough course with the heat," Elson told the *Ottawa Citizen*. "It was not my best time, but I am thrilled to do it in this heat."

1982

A PRINCE IS BORN

William, son of the Prince and Princess of Wales, was born in London, and became second in line to the throne.

INSTANT BATH

Jean Lariault of Hull, Quebec was doused with water at the end of a hot race.

EIGHT AND COUNTING

Running partners **Arthur Monsebraaten** and **Garry Bowes** of Ottawa ran together in 1982. Bowes went on to complete all of the first 20 editions of the Ottawa Marathon.

E.T. LIGHTS IT UP

E.T. the Extra-Terrestrial, co-produced and directed by Steven Spielberg, hit theatres.

Man getting into motion

4,658
marathon participants

+20c

2:21:37
Mike Dyon
Men's Winner

2:54:13
Celia McInnis
Women's Winner

When he arrived at the start line of the Ottawa Marathon in 1983, Rick Hansen had already begun to prepare for his Man in Motion World Tour, the historic 40,000-kilometre journey that would begin in less than two years.

"It had been a wild and crazy dream for many years," he says, "but now I was starting to believe that it was possible."

His plans to wheel around the world were starting to get serious. But first, Hansen had plenty of racing left to do as an elite athlete. As well as competing in Ottawa, he planned to do marathons in Toronto and Montreal that year. He also intended to enter the inaugural marathon at the 1984 Paralympic Games in the United Kingdom, and the first-ever exhibition event for wheelchair athletes at the 1984 Summer Olympics in Los Angeles.

Like many other athletes, Hansen saw the marathon as a personal test. He was also a favourite every time he raced. A CBC camera crew followed him to Ottawa, documenting his every move. But as an athlete in a sport that was only just opening up to people with disabilities, every event was also about knocking down barriers and achieving new levels of inclusion.

"The experience of representing my country in sport made me see the injustice that people with disabilities faced: being marginalized, stereotyped, discriminated against," he says. "That became the motivation to do a physical journey that would remove those barriers."

After suffering a spinal cord injury when he was 15, Hansen became a world-class wheelchair basketball player, and later convinced Terry Fox to take up the sport. He started competing in track and road-racing events because he enjoyed the fitness training he was doing for basketball, and migrated to the marathon when he discovered he had a high level of endurance.

Hansen won gold, silver, and bronze medals in middle-distance and relay events at the 1980 Paralympic Games. He was the first wheelchair athlete across the finish line at the 1982 Boston Marathon, and went on to win 19 marathons, including three world championships.

Hansen remembers the Ottawa course being picturesque and historic. "The setting was outstanding," he says.

Wheelchair athletes had participated in the Ottawa Marathon before, but 1983 was the first year they were given a separate division and encouraged to enter, so Hansen was the first official winner in the category.

"It was such a golden time in the sport," he says.

But even then, inclusion wasn't universal for wheelchair athletes. The venerable New York City Marathon fought a series of legal battles with athletes with disabilities before finally allowing them into the race and then establishing a separate division in 2000. That's why Hansen sees the 1983 Ottawa Marathon in historic terms.

"The fact that the marathon in my nation's capital was opening its doors to wheelchair athletes had huge symbolism," he says. "Sport is a mirror for how society views itself, for its values. If the Ottawa Marathon is inclusive and accommodating, then so is the city, and, given it's the nation's capital, then, so is our country."

Hansen gives credit to the race organizers who led the way to creating a wheelchair division. "They had the foresight to allow it to take place," he says. "It doesn't just happen. It takes people who have those values. That's how you build an event, and how you build a country."

And even though more than 30 years has passed since the first wheelchair race in Ottawa, Hansen says the work isn't over.

"We still have more to do to follow the lead of the Ottawa Marathon and build an even more accessible national capital, and build a country that's free of barriers and inclusive for all."

> The fact that the marathon in my nation's capital was opening its doors to wheelchair athletes had huge symbolism.

RICK HANSEN

![Labatt's Lite National Capital Marathon '83 logo]

LABATT'S LITE NATIONAL CAPITAL MARATHON '83

NEW LOGO

The Ottawa Marathon adopted a new logo this year. The Secretary of State asked marathon organizers to drop the old logo that showed a runner on a Canadian flag because it was too similar to the national flag. The new logo featured a striding runner with the Peace Tower in the background.

HITTING THE WALL

Anne Murphy, 23, ran her second marathon and first in Ottawa. "What I remember most about it was hitting the wall with about 10 kilometres left. I was on pace to do a 3:30 marathon, but had to run-walk the last bit, and ended up with a 3:45." Murphy didn't run another marathon until she turned 50 in 2010.

SPRINT TO THE FINISH

Celia McInnis won her first marathon. At the 30-kilometre mark she sat in fifth place, but she slowly moved her way up the pack, passing the 1981 winner, Kathy Needham Tanner, and two other runners. It was not until the finishing stretch at Carleton University that she caught sight of the leader, Tracey Robinson, McInnis's teammate from the Waterloo County Amateur Athletic Association. "I put on my best sprint, and passed her within 100 meters of the finish," remembers McInnis. "I enjoyed the race a great deal, but sprinting at the end of a marathon is not easy, or maybe it's that stopping after sprinting at the end of a marathon is not easy. After the finish line, when I had to stop, there was an incredible amount of lactic acid in my legs – a couple of volunteers fortunately grabbed me or I might have toppled."

FROM YOUNGEST TO OLDEST

The youngest participant was 10-year-old Claire Beland of Engelhard, Ontario. The oldest male was George Capraru, 71, of Toronto, and, once again 63-year-old **Judith Kazdan** of Willowdale, Ontario was the oldest female.

FOUR MORE...

The 20-Minute Workout brought fitness to Canadian TV screens.

3-2-1

The first flight of the Space Shuttle Challenger was launched from Cape Canaveral.

7:1

There were 3,976 male runners and 592 female participants in the Ottawa Marathon, with 21 under the age of 15.

1983

THE ORIGINAL BEER RUN

The race was renamed the Labatt's Lite National Capital Marathon. The race featured 10 timing, eight water, and seven sponge stations along the course. A nurse was available at each refreshment station, and a fully equipped medical van was on hand for emergencies. For the first time, the leading woman received a bicycle escort, and was able to break special tape at the finish.

TECH TIMING

At the finish line, a $3,700 double-sided digital clock was added. It was a first in Canada.

HIDDEN ACCESSIBILITY

Ottawa Sports Hall of Fame inductee **Jacques Pilon** became the first blind runner to finish the Ottawa Marathon in under three hours. He told the *Ottawa Citizen* in 1992 that he liked the race because it's a flat course. Pilon remembered his long training days in 1983, when he ran up and down 273 steps at the YMCA 29 times, and did a similar workout on the ramps of the Ottawa Civic Centre. Pilon, who captured gold in the 1980 Blind Olympics, said he was grateful for those two examples of Ottawa's "hidden accessibilities" that allowed him to train as a disabled athlete."

CABBAGE PATCH CRAZINESS

Parents across North America stood in huge lines and frantically searched everywhere for the coveted Cabbage Patch Kids dolls.

CANADA, EH?

Strange Brew, featuring the popular SCTV characters **Bob and Doug McKenzie** and starring Dave Thomas and Rick Moranis, was released.

A noteworthy debut

MAY

13

3,740

marathon participants

☿ **+15c**

2:13:19

Dave Edge

Men's Winner

2:30:37

Silvia Ruegger

Women's Winner

On September 11, 1976, just a few weeks after the Summer Olympics in Montreal, 15-year-old Silvia Ruegger wrote herself a note and tucked it under the loose floorboards of her family's farmhouse in rural Ontario.

Ruegger carefully concealed the hole with masking tape and pulled a carpet across the spot. She never removed the note from its hiding place to look at it again, but it fuelled her ambition for the next eight years.

The note set out an audacious goal: to run for Canada at the Olympics. And in May 1984, in Ottawa, she fulfilled the first part of that objective. Ruegger ran the first marathon of her life, the Olympic qualifying race, and won, earning a ticket to the Summer Games in Los Angeles.

"Just crossing the finish line was the dream come true," says Ruegger.

Ruegger had never planned to be a distance runner, because there was no Olympic marathon for women. In late 1983, after recovering from a series of injuries that had stalled her track career for more than two years, she ran a 10k race in San Diego and heard from a reporter about the plans to add a women's marathon to the Olympics the following summer.

"Wow, there's going to be a women's marathon," she remembers thinking. "When I heard that, I knew I had to be there."

But Ruegger had only a few months to prepare for the qualifying race in Ottawa, which would be her first marathon. She contacted running coach Hugh Cameron and convinced him to help her.

They met for the first time on January 7, 1984. To this day she wonders why Cameron didn't tell her to aim for the Olympic marathon in four years rather than try for the qualifying event in just four months. But he put together the program that prepared her for Ottawa.

In fact, the training schedule he created went all the way up to the Olympic Marathon in August.

Against a strong field of Olympic hopefuls in Ottawa, Ruegger executed her race plan perfectly. She broke away at 30 kilometres and led the race the rest of the way. Her time was the fastest ever for a debut marathon by a woman.

When she crossed the finish line, one of her first thoughts was of her mother. When Ruegger trained on country roads as a teenager, her mother got up every morning to follow her in the car.

"You don't have streetlights in the country," says Ruegger. "I would get up needing to run before school. And she would get behind me and drive with the headlights on because that was the only light I had.

"For her to do that at that time was amazing," she says. "Women's running was not encouraged at the time. She took more flak than I did. People said, 'You're encouraging her.' But she saw the passion and wanted to do whatever she could to help me. She was 'way ahead of her time."

In Los Angeles, Ruegger finished eighth in only her second marathon, and set a Canadian record.

On the night she packed for the Summer Olympics, Ruegger's mother asked her if she remembered the note she wrote to herself.

"I was shocked that she knew about it," says Ruegger. "She said she had found it, probably a few years after I wrote it. She said she thought, 'There is a girl who has some pretty high goals.' And she put the note back in the floor exactly as she had found it."

Ruegger says when she wrote the note, she never expected to be a marathon runner. But she's grateful the doors opened for her at just the right time.

"When I had that dream to be an Olympian I had no idea how it was going to happen," she says. "I was injured for a long time, and never gave up on my dream. Delay does not mean denial.

"And when people ask me about the most exciting moments in my career, of course I always think of the Olympics. But for me, Ottawa was really special. It's where my dream came true."

> "Just crossing the finish line was the dream come true."

SILVIA RUEGGER

LABATT'S NATIONAL CAPITAL MARATHON 1984 DE LA CAPITALE NATIONALE

FIRST AMONG FIRSTS

The women's marathon was introduced at the 1984 Summer Olympics and was won by **Joan Benoit** of the United States with a time of 2:24:52. Forty-four women competed in the event.

SECOND BEST

Anne-Marie Malone had to settle for second after Silvia Reugger took off just after the 20-mile mark.

HOP TO IT

Ottawa's **Mark Wigmore** ran his second Ottawa marathon. He became a pace bunny in 2006 and then took over organizing the pace bunnies in 2008.

UNPLANNED PIT STOP

Past Ottawa winner and Olympian **Wayne Yetman** started the 1984 marathon, but didn't finish the race. "I was running along, feeling pretty bad, and decided, 'No more pain for me,'" he told the *Ottawa Citizen* in 1985. "So at about 20 miles, I made a little detour into the Chateau Laurier and sat there drinking beer for the rest of the day."

325 AND COUNTING

Sy Mah, a Canadian-born professor at the University of Toledo, finished his 325th marathon in a time of 3:37. Mah formed the Metro Toronto Fitness Club and the North York Track Club. In 1967, at the age of 41, he ran his first marathon. He went on to average 20 marathons a year. When he died in 1988, he had run a record 524 marathons. His standard stood until 1994.

HUNGRY BUNCH

At the finish line, runners consumed 4,000 bananas, 3,000 oranges, and a truckload of yogurt in five different flavours.

1984

END OF AN ERA

Canada said goodbye to the stubby beer bottle.

SUPER MARIO

The Pittsburgh Penguins selected **Mario Lemieux** with the first pick of the NHL Entry Draft. On October 11, Lemieux scored his first NHL goal in his first game, on his first shift.

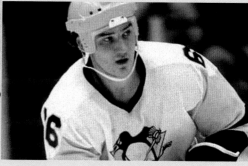

CELEBRATING AT THE FINISH

Art Boileau, who finished third, **Alain Bordeleau**, who was second, and winner **Dave Edge**, were greeted by Canadian Track and Field president **Bill McNutty**.

BEFORE MODERN CONVENIENCES

Diana King remembers what marathons were like before technology took over. "In the early days," she says, "energy drinks, power bars, and energy gels hadn't been invented yet. Only water was handed out at the water stations." She remembers a friend who had his wife hand him a cup of flat Coke near the final stretch of the race. "He knew from experience that he needed the energy boost for the for the last 10 kilometres." King continues, "There were no pace bunnies, GPS watches, iPods, heart monitors, or anything that you could pre-program to practically run your race for you. Serious runners wrote their desired splits on their wrists, on a piece of paper, or even memorized them and just went for it." King has run seven Ottawa Marathons and 10 half-marathons since 1983.

ON TO L.A.

The 1984 Ottawa Marathon was the trial race for Canada's Olympic team. The top three male and top two female finishers went on to represent Canada in Los Angeles. **Dave Edge** of Burlington, Ontario eclipsed the course record by almost three minutes. Edge stayed with the pack for the first 33 kilometres, before taking the lead at the corner of Wellington Street and Colonel By Drive. His tactic frustrated some of the front-runners – it's an unwritten rule for the top runners to take turns leading the pack. But Edge dismissed the complaints at the time: "Why would I take the lead? It is kind of silly. The pack was fun, slow and steady."

1985

MAY
12

2,600
marathon participants

☀

🌡 +20c

2:16:18
Ric Sayre
Men's Winner

2:47:56
Marian Teitsch
Women's Winner

A life-changing photograph

In May 1975, Diane Palmason picked up a copy of the *Ottawa Citizen* and flipped to the sports section. The photo on the front page showed Eleanor Thomas, the first woman to cross the finish line at the inaugural Ottawa Marathon.

"That picture changed my life," says Palmason.

Palmason set her mind to running the Ottawa Marathon the next year. And she didn't stop there. She ran Ottawa almost every year until 1985. Over the last 40 years, Palmason has completed 78 marathons, has set countless Masters and age group records, and is a member of the Canadian Road Running Hall of Fame.

It's a passion she never expected to cultivate. As a high school track athlete in the 1950s, Palmason had been taught that women shouldn't run long distances. Until 1960, the farthest women could race in the Olympics was 200 metres.

"I loved to run," she says. "And I always thought I could run farther with the boys, but I wasn't allowed to."

Although she was strong enough at track to represent Canada at the 1954 Commonwealth Games, Palmason always suspected she would do better at longer distances. But since that opportunity didn't exist for women, she gave up running when she went to university, and then had four children in seven years.

"In the 1950s, it was, 'Okay, women, go back into the kitchen,'" she says. "There just was not a culture of rebelling and saying we're going to do this anyway. That didn't start until the 1960s. And by that time I had four kids, and I had other things on my mind."

She did run occasionally, but she says in those days it wasn't considered acceptable to run outside. So she often ran in circles around her house.

"Or I would wait until it was dark and then I would get the dog and put her on leash and run on the streets. If a car came along, I would stop. Once it passed, I would start again."

Everything changed when she saw the photo.

"I had grown up with the impression that girls don't do that. Women don't run more than 220 yards. Here was this woman who had just run 26 miles."

Palmason remembers thinking, "Oh, I want to do that." She says, "It was just like that. It was highly irrational, in many ways."

That's especially true because she was recovering from back surgery, and her doctor was not excited about the prospect of her running long distances.

"He said, 'Forget it, you're not going to be able to run,'" she says. "Needless to say, I didn't pay much attention to him."

As she prepared for her first marathon in 1976, her first call was to Thomas.

"I phoned Eleanor and I said, 'You don't know me, but I saw your picture in the paper,'" says Palmason. "'I've never run a marathon. I've never run any road race. What do I wear? What happens if I have to go to the bathroom?' She was immensely patient and helpful."

Over the next few years, Palmason won various trophies and awards for her performances in Ottawa, including trips to other marathons. But in those days there, weren't big cash prizes for the winners, let alone Masters athletes.

"I have a wooden thing that's a clock for being the first Masters woman in 1979," she says. "Only the clock doesn't work. And from 1981, I have something that's kind of like a desk set. Over in one corner, there's a figurine of a woman running in a style that would have gotten her once around the track, but not to the finish line of a marathon."

That changed in 1985. Palmason wasn't planning to run Ottawa that year until a few weeks before the event when she ran into one of the organizers.

"She said, 'You're not registered this year,'" says Palmason. "'I said, 'No, I don't think I'm going to run it.' And she said, 'Well, there's $3,000 for the first Canadian woman.'"

Palmason had been training for a 1,500-metre race. So she asked friends for advice. One told her to forget the marathon – advice that she once again ignored. Another told her to get lots of rest. She ran the race and won the cash prize.

Palmason ended up setting a number of world records, including some that she still holds to this day. She took up coaching – running became a vocation as well as an avocation, she says. And it all started with a photo from the first Ottawa Marathon.

"I was literally in the right place at the right time," she says.

"I loved to run. And I always thought I could run farther with the boys, but I wasn't allowed to."

DIANE PALMASON

RELIEF FROM THE HEAT

It was a hot and humid marathon, with the temperature at some points of the course reaching as high as 27C. To help competitors cool off, race volunteers handed out sponges along the Parkway.

LONG ROAD BACK

Hamilton's **Bruce Wainman**, a future Ottawa champion, ran his first marathon in six years. He was the top Canadian finisher, coming in third overall in 2:21:23. See his story in 1986.

GLOBAL JUKEBOX

Live Aid concerts in Philadelphia and London on July 13, 1985 were watched by an estimated 1.9 billion people and raised more than $50 million for famine relief in Ethiopia. The shows followed the release in January of USA for Africa's "We Are the World," a charity single featuring some of the most successful American artists of the time.

A SPRING TRADITION

Matthew Grasmeyer made the drive from Barrie, Ontario to Ottawa to run his firs marathon in 1977, when he was just 18 years old. When he moved to Ottawa in 1981 the race became an annual tradition for Grasmeyer. He placed 9th overall in 1985, hi best placing ever. In 1992, he ran his last Ottawa marathon, coming 9th once again ir a time of 2:39:37. "I did that one on memories, not training," says Grasmeyer. "I jus thought I better run one last one." But he admits that after it was over, he decide that maybe a little training might have been a good idea.

SO LONG

The last episode of the popular Canadian children's television program *The Friendly Giant* appeared on CBC Television after 27 years on the air.

NOT SO FOOLISH AFTER ALL

Larry McCloskey was determined to stay with the leaders when he ran his third Ottawa Marathon, but he says he was left in their dust right from the start. "Not fast enough to stay with the lead and not slow enough to have anyone to run with," he says. "So I ran 41 kilometers by myself, and finished 3rd in 2:24." McCloskey says he was pleased with the placing, but disappointed with the time. And he remembers the circumstances 10 years earlier that inspired him to run his first marathon. "My father and I happened to be driving through Carleton University as the runners were lining up to begin the marathon, and through the cloud of smoke that was a constant in my father's car, I thought, 'Maybe I could try that," just as my dad made one of his rare pronouncements: 'Grown men doing that—how foolish!'"

1985

AGENT OF CHANGE

Mikhail Gorbachev replaced Konstantin Chernenko as the leader of the Soviet Union.

AMERICAN SWEEP

American runners took the top men's and women's spots for the second time. **Ric Sayre** of Oregon won the men's marathon, leading the race from start to finish. The next year, Sayre won the inaugural Los Angeles Marathon with a personal best of 2:12:09. In 1987, Sayre captured the U.S. national marathon champion-   ship. Sayre died in 2011 at the   age of 56. He won 12 of the 50 marathons he entered during his career.

BIKE ESCORT

Women's winner Marian Teitsch had some company during her 42.2-kilometre run. Vicki Alwyen-Smith was beside her every step of the way. Alwyn-Smith, a member of the Gloucester Cycling Club, was assigned by the race committee to escort the women's race leader. "The cyclist was extremely helpful," said Teitsch in an interview with the *Ottawa Citizen*. "She encouraged me with her words. She was just great. I wish I knew her name." Alwyn-Smith's words of encouragement came in particularly handy at the 32-kilometre mark, when Teitsch said she started to get stomach cramps.

TEENAGE CHAMP

Unseeded Boris Becker became the youngest player ever to win the Wimbledon men's title, at the age of 17.

1986

"So much bloody fun it was ridiculous"

The last few kilometres of a marathon are almost always challenging. They can also be devastating and demoralizing, or life-affirming and empowering. But they are rarely described as fun.

Yet Bruce Wainman was having a pretty good time as he ran the final stretch of the Ottawa Marathon in 1986.

"I was having so much bloody fun it was ridiculous," says Wainman, who won the race in two hours and eighteen minutes.

According to an account in the *Ottawa Citizen*, Wainman high-fived spectators, squirted water at children and even waved at the football cheerleaders on the sideline.

Today he remembers everything but the cheerleaders. But he admits it's probably true. "Had they been there, I would have done that," he says.

After breaking away from the lead pack, Wainman ran by himself for the entire second half of the race. But he wasn't happy just because he was going to win. He was glad to be healthy after injuries almost convinced him he would never run fast again.

Despite being a future marathon champion, Wainman didn't make his school's cross-country team when he tried out in Grade 8. But he kept running and discovered a natural talent.

"One day I just decided to start running, and it felt like the easiest thing in the world to do," he says. "All of a sudden it just felt like I was doing the right thing."

Wainman found that the farther he ran, the better he performed. So he ran a few marathons as a teenager, and then went on to a successful athletic career at university.

But as he tried to improve his speed, he suffered a serious injury to his ankle. "I pretty much gave up on running very fast," he says.

After several months of rest, however, the ankle started to improve, and Wainman started working with a new coach. In 1985, he ran Ottawa and finished third. "I looked like death," he says of the finish of the race, a sharp contrast to what happened the following year.

The race was an important test. He felt like he had been given a second chance.

"I'd been so injured, I never thought I'd be able to come back," says Wainman. "Getting hurt was the best thing that ever happened to me. When I came back, I realized how really fortunate you are. When you're a kid, you think it's always going to be like this. But now I could really appreciate how great it was to be able to run."

That's why he enjoyed Ottawa, so much in 1986. "I was so happy to feel so good," he says. "I never had so much fun in a race. I don't think I ever felt that good again."

He later heard from a spectator who was inspired to run the marathon by seeing how much Wainman seemed to be enjoying the race.

"Some guy came up to me and said, 'I saw you running in Ottawa and it looked like you were having so much fun,'" he says. "And it's actually not that much fun at all.'"

Wainman ran a few more marathons before succumbing to injuries again. He still runs regularly, but rarely for long distances.

It's far enough in the past that his son once dug out an old scrapbook and was surprised to find pictures of his father winning races.

"He was about seven or eight at the time," says Wainman. "And he said, 'Dad, you used to be Bruce Wainman!' Yeah, that's who I used to be."

Almost 30 years has passed, but the memories of his win in Ottawa, and especially that final stretch during which he celebrated with the crowd, are still very vivid.

"I'll go to Ottawa for meetings," he says, "And I'll be running along the canal and I'll just have that weird feeling of being back there.

"I forget so many things, but I can't forget that. It's burned into my mind."

> I never had so much fun in a race. I don't think I ever felt that good again.

BRUCE WAINMAN

POWERING THROUGH

PowerBar was founded in 1986 in Berkeley, California by **Mike McCollum** and **Brian Maxwell**, a Canadian athlete and entrepreneur and winner of the 1979 Ottawa Marathon. The partners came up with the recipe along with Maxwell's future wife Jennifer. They used $55,000 in cash to launch the company.

PowerBar

GRETE THE GREAT

For the second time, **Grete Waitz** won both the London and New York City marathons in the same year. She also accomplished the feat in 1983.

FERGIE FEVER BEGINS

Prince Andrew and **Sarah Ferguson** married on March 17, 1986 at Westminster Abbey.

ROCK RIGHTS

"(You Gotta) Fight for Your Right (to Party!)" by the Beastie Boys became the rock anthem of the late 80s.

FINISHING IN THE MONEY

Olympic cross-country skier **Joan Groothuysen** won the Ottawa Marathon, but about five kilometres from the finish line, she was struggling to stay on pace to hit the time of 2:55 required to qualify for prize money. "Under the Bronson Bridge I was so tired, I just didn't give a damn," she told the *Ottawa Citizen* at the time. "But when I got to University Drive, I knew I was going to make it." Groothuysen represented Canada at the 1976 and 1980 Winter Olympics. In order to maintain her amateur status, her Ottawa prize money was kept in trust.

SITCOM SUCCESS

A furry brown alien named *Alf* became a primetime TV hit.

DOWN BUT NOT OUT

The Ottawa Marathon almost didn't happen in 1986. Just six weeks before the race, the board of directors voted to cancel the event. Participation in running events was declining, and Ottawa was facing competition from a new spring marathon in Montreal. The race was having trouble attracting sponsors and was turned down by 23 different companies for liability insurance. But after the announcement, new sponsors stepped forward and insurance was secured from a group of providers in the U.S. The community, Parker said at the time, "simply wouldn't let the race die."

A WEEKEND IS BORN

In an effort to expand the event and boost participation, organizers added a 10k race to the marathon. Race director Ken Parker told the *Ottawa Citizen* that with interest in the marathon declining, it made sense to add a shorter distance. In the first year, the 10k attracted just over half the number of runners as the marathon, but as Parker predicted, it soon grew to be much larger. But interest in the marathon soon recovered and both events became anchors of the new Ottawa Race Weekend.

COFFEY BREAK

Paul Coffey of the Edmonton Oilers scored his 47th and 48th goals of the season in an 8-4 win against Vancouver to break Bobby Orr's NHL record for most goals by a defenceman. The Oilers went on to win the 1986 Stanley Cup.

"Under the Bronson Bridge I was so tired, I just didn't give a damn. But when I got to University Drive, I knew I was going to make it."

Joan Groothuysen

"Are you going to be strong today?"

MAY
10

1,210
marathon participants

🌡 **+20c**

2:12:58
Peter Maher
Men's Winner

2:40:59
Dorothy Goertzen
Women's Winner

2,700
Race Weekend participants

In August 1983, Peter Maher was a long way from running – let alone winning – the Ottawa Marathon. For one thing, the Ottawa native was thousands of miles away, living, working and raising a family in his ancestral home of Ireland.

Not only that, Maher weighed 250 pounds and smoked a couple of packs of cigarettes every day.

After his family moved back to Ireland from Canada when he was a child, Maher became a star runner as a teenager, winning several national titles and earning an athletic scholarship to East Tennessee State University. But he suffered a partial tear of his Achilles tendon, and it cost him his spot in university athletics.

"I felt really hard done-by," he says. "So I partied hard for about five years, smoking, drinking, and putting on an enormous amount of weight."

Maher says it got so bad that he didn't enjoy looking at himself in the mirror. So in 1983 he said, "I'm not doing this anymore."

"I walked away from the drinking buddies," he says. "I came to terms with myself, and decided I was going to start running again. The first time I tried, the farthest I could go was about 20 metres."

Maher says he lost much of his weight very quickly when he began running again. But he never expected it to lead to a career as an elite marathoner.

"I never, ever, ever dreamed I would go on and do the things I did," he says. "I was just trying to get some form of control over my life."

He soon moved back to Canada and began training seriously for longer distances. His performances improved by leaps and bounds, and after he posted a fast time in the Around the Bay 30-kilometre race in Hamilton, his coach suggested he run Ottawa.

Not only did he win, but he set a new course record of 2:12:58, eclipsing Dave Edge's time from the talent-rich, Olympic-qualifying 1984 marathon. Maher's record stood for 17 years.

"When people ask me what are the biggest performances in my life," he says, "I put Ottawa right up there. It gave me great belief that I could run at the international level, and ultimately the Olympics. It was really the launching pad of my career as a runner."

Maher went on to win many other races and represented Canada in the Olympic marathon in 1988 and 1992, and at the world championships four times. He set a world record in the 25k in 1991.

Along the way, the loquacious athlete became the source of a quote about running that has been repeated often. Maher once said, "Running is a big question mark that's there each and every day. It asks you, 'Are you going to be a wimp, or are you going to be strong today?'"

The inspiration for those words came when Maher was in Florida and facing heat and humidity for a training run. "Nobody's going to tell you to go out," he remembers thinking to himself. "Are you going to be a champ or are you going to be a wimp? It's your call."

Training for the marathon, he says, was the perfect way to answer the question.

"The more you physically challenge yourself to be uncomfortable, the more you grow mentally," he says. "It forces you to go to places that you don't normally go in our comfortable society. That's available to everybody who undertakes a marathon. That's the beauty of the event."

When his competitive career was over, Maher moved back to Ireland, where today he runs his own sports therapy business. Running now fills a different role in his life.

"For me running is now a tranquilizer and a spiritual journey," he says. "It's heavily laden with spirituality."

Looking back on a successful career, the two-time Olympian says Ottawa stands out as one of his best races and most powerful memories.

"There's just no words to describe going back to the city you were born in, winning the marathon, and breaking the course record," says Maher. "It's like a story you've made up."

"
For me running is
now a tranquilizer and
a spiritual journey.

PETER MAHER
"

PUMPING IT UP

Nike launched the *Air Max*, the first Nike footwear to feature visible air bags. The marketing campaign was supported by a memorable TV ad with a soundtrack using the original Beatles' recording of "Revolution."

WAR STORIES

Oliver North was summoned to testify before televised hearings of a joint Congressional committee formed to investigate the Iran–Contra Affair.

THE WEST WANTS IN

Preston Manning became the first leader of the Reform Party of Canada.

PERENNIAL PLAYER

Larry McCloskey ran the marathon for the fifth year in a row. After watching the 1980 marathon from the sidelines, McCloskey decided to try it himself the next year, running his first marathon in 1981 in 3:15. In 1984, he finished 17th with a personal best of 2.24. McCloskey, shown here with his running partner of 20 years Matthew Grasmeyer, ran the Ottawa marathon every year until 1989, when he switched over to the 10k race.

A PROLIFIC DECADE

Doug Smith started running in 1978 and ran a total of 23 marathons in the 1980s. In 1984, he ran the Ottawa Marathon in 3:01, placing 500th. He returned again in 1987. "I really enjoyed the race and the chance to run by my Parliament Buildings and along the canal," he says. Smith is now president of Ontario Masters Athletics, and is still running, but no longer competes in marathons.

IN THE LEAD

Eventual winner **Peter Maher** was ahead of the pack early in the race.

WELCOME TO SPRINGFIELD

On April 19, 1987, Bart, Homer, Lisa, Marge, and Maggie Simpson appeared on North American TV screens for the first time. *The Simpsons* began as a short on the Tracy Ullman Show.

1987

WINNING GAMBLE

A week before the 1987 marathon, **Dorothy Goertzen** didn't even think she would be up for running the 42.2 kilometres because of what she thought was a stress fracture. It turned out to be tendinitis in the fibula, and it didn't stop her from winning the women's event in 2:40:59. "This is a miracle," the 31-year-old told the *Ottawa Citizen* after the race. "Sometimes it's worth a little gamble."

CROSSING THE DIVIDE

American **Lynne Cox** became the first person to swim from the United States to the Soviet Union. She took two hours and six minutes to cross the Bering Strait, which separates the Arctic and Pacific Oceans and the world's two superpowers.

OPENING UP

Negotiators completed the Canada-U.S. Free Trade Agreement.

"The beautiful and well-laid-out course, the frequent water and sponge stops, the abundant medical help (which, luckily, I didn't need...!), beautiful weather, and enthusiastic volunteers and spectators made this race a memorable experience. It was well worth the trip from Nova Scotia, and you can be sure I'll be back next year."

Davender Gupta of Berwick, Nova Scotia, in a letter to the *Ottawa Citizen*.

1988

All in the family

MAY
8

1,477
marathon participants

🌡 +18c

2:18:40
Gord Christie
Men's Winner

2:52:08
Margarita Galicia
Women's Winner

3,267
Race Weekend participants

After each of them had completed several marathons, Ken and Sandra Malloy decided in 1987 that they would start running shorter distances.

"Up to that time, I had run 10 marathons and Sandra had run four," says Ken. "We decided that was enough and that we wanted to do just 10k races from then on. We said, 'That's it, we're finished doing marathons.'"

But their three sons had other ideas. Peter, Sean, and Kevin Malloy weren't long-distance runners, but they were all in pretty good shape, playing competitively with the Ottawa Irish Rugby Club.

"They came to us and asked if we'd do one more and we'd all do it as a family," says Ken. "They talked us into it. We said, 'Okay, we'll do one more.'"

So in 1988, all five members of the family registered for the Ottawa Marathon.

"We thought it would be a cool thing to do," says Kevin Malloy, who was 21 at the time. "We always watched our parents run. So we figured we should see if we could do a marathon together."

Kevin remembers the Ottawa Marathon as an annual event in his family. He and his brothers would watch his father run every May. And after a few years, his mother started running it too.

"We always went to Carleton U to watch him finish," says Kevin. "My dad did five or six before my mom started running. She started running them in her 40s, and she loved it right away. They would run together all the time. But she was a bit faster than him."

In those days, the marathon was held on Mother's Day. So the family would gather for the marathon and then go out for a meal.

"That's the way we celebrated Mother's Day," says Ken.

As all five members of the family started training for the 1988 marathon, it was only natural that a friendly rivalry developed among the brothers, who were all in their 20s.

"It was a big competition to see who would finish first," says Kevin. Just a few days before the race, he told the *Ottawa Citizen*, "My goal is to beat my brothers."

On race day, Ken says, a few members of the family started the race with aches and pains, and Peter had previously had knee surgery for a rugby injury. But there was no chance any of them would fail to cross the finish line.

"If one of us didn't finish, they'd still be bugging us about it to this day," he says. "You'd never be allowed to forget it."

At a turnaround point about halfway through the race, Kevin and Sean were running together, ahead of their older brother.

"Finally we saw Pete and started pointing at him and laughing," says Kevin. "He wasn't too happy about that."

Sean was the first member of the family to cross the finish line, followed by Kevin, Sandra, Ken and Peter.

"The main thing was that Sean and I beat my mom," says Kevin. "But it was the hardest thing ever. I wanted to quit so many times. But when we all finished, it was awesome."

As usual, the family celebrated by going out for a Mother's Day meal.

Kevin went on to run another four marathons, and has also completed several triathlons, including three Ironmans. Peter has done triathlons as well, and Sean has competed in duathlons. As for Ken and Sandra, they retired from the marathon, one race later than they had originally planned.

"That was it," says Ken. "That was our swan song."

More than 25 years later, the Malloys still have a photo from the race on the wall of their home.

"We were all very happy to do it," says Ken. "And Sandra and I were very proud that they asked us to run together."

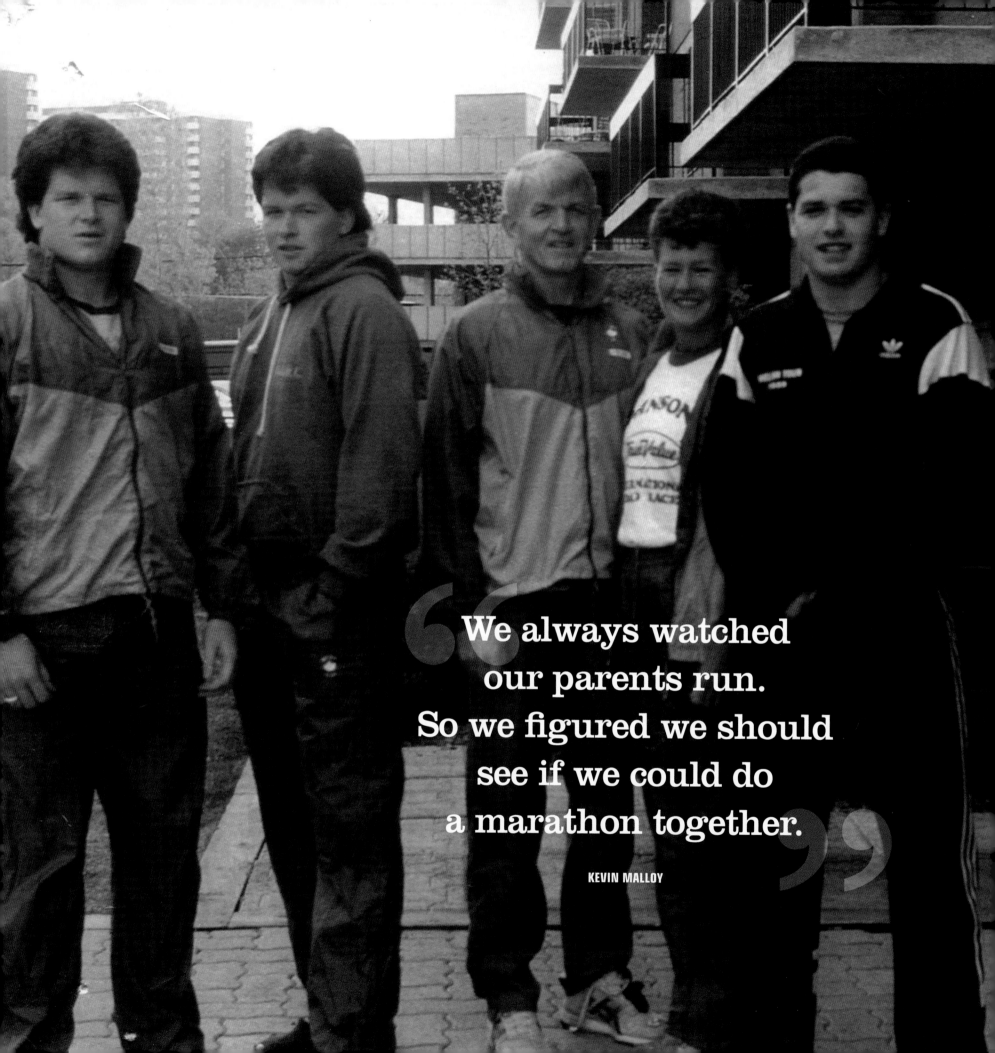

> "We always watched our parents run. So we figured we should see if we could do a marathon together."

KEVIN MALLOY

42 PLUS 10

The marathon wasn't always enough for 64-year-old **Andy Taylor** of Smiths Falls, Ontario. Taylor often ran the 10k on Saturday as a way of warming up for the marathon on Sunday morning. He started running as a boy in Scotland, racing everything from the mile to the steeplechase to the marathon. Taylor moved from Scotland to Canada in 1966, ultimately settling in Smiths Falls. He soon bumped into Ottawa runner Danny Daniels, whom he had known as a teenager back in Scotland. "I think they recognized each other's ugly running style 60 years later," jokes his son Ken Taylor. Daniels convinced Taylor to start running competitively, and he never stopped. Taylor ran his first Ottawa Marathon in 1979 and ran his last competitive race when he was 79-years-old. Taylor died in September 2013.

STRICT RULES

Bernard Voyer of Hull finished second in the marathon, but was later disqualified for accepting a drink from a non-designated water station. He appealed his decision to the Canadian Track and Field Association, but lost.

HOMECOMING KING

A native of Inuvik who lived in Ottawa for three years as a child, **Gord Christie** won his first of three Ottawa Marathons in a row.

1988

FATHER'S DAY
Michael Petrocci of St. Catharines, Ontario may not have won the marathon in 1988 (as he did in 1991 and 1992) but it was still a special race. Petrocci's father had been suffering from a progressive neurological illness, but both of the runner's parents watched the race from along Colonel By Drive. After he finished third, Petrocci secured the help of a race volunteer and picked up his parents so they could all be together in the finish area.

LA GANADORA
Margarita Galicia, of Mexico, became the first, and only, Mexican to win the marathon in the race's 40-year history.

THE CHAMP
21-year-old Mike Tyson knocked out Michael Spinks 91 seconds into the first round to become the undisputed heavyweight champion of the world.

CLOSE FINISH
Italy's Gelindo Bordin passed Kenya's Douglas Wakiihuri in the last two kilometres of the men's Olympic marathon in Seoul, South Korea. Bordin held on to win the gold medal, but the 15-second margin between the runners was the smallest in an Olympic marathon since 1920.

AT LONG LAST
Barry Roman of Kirkland, Quebec was the 1,219th, and last, to complete the race. He crossed the finish line five hours, 38 minutes, and 17 seconds after the race started.

FRENCH DRAMA
Canadian cyclist **Steve Bauer** won the first stage of the Tour de France and wore the Yellow Jersey for five days.

At last, the finish line

MAY 14

1,046
marathon participants

+21c

2:14:33
Gord Christie
Men's Winner

2:44:58
Lisa Bouchard
Women's Winner

2,400
Race Weekend participants

In the second half of the 1989 Ottawa Marathon, Debbie Wyllie watched as other runners at the back of the pack pulled themselves out of the race and boarded the bus that would take them to the finish line.

"I was kind of hard-headed, I guess," says Wyllie. "So I wasn't going to quit."

Although she found it painful at times, Wyllie kept going. She remembers being passed somewhere near the finish line by another woman who was limping.

"She ran past me and I thought, 'Oh God, what's wrong with me?'" she says.

The result is that Wyllie had the distinction of being the last person to complete the race, finishing in just over six hours.

"I was the last one that hadn't jumped on the bus," she says. "They actually kept the course open for me. It was really awesome."

A year before the marathon, Wyllie joined the running club at Nortel, the company she worked for in Brampton, Ontario.

"Sometimes you're in a place in your life when you need a change, to do something different," she says.

She was quickly hooked on the new activity. "You're just on such a high when you run," she says. "You really do feel good. You feel high on life."

After training "like a maniac" for six weeks, Wyllie ran her first 10k. The group went on to enter other races around Ontario. Then a co-worker who had seen both his parents suffer from Alzheimer's disease invited her to join him and a few others in running a marathon as a fundraiser for medical research.

Nortel agreed to match any donations, and the group of five runners set about training and soliciting donations. They ended up collecting more than $5,000 for the cause.

Wyllie knew she wasn't going to finish the race quickly. But she'd had some recent foot injuries, and a doctor had even advised her to consider skipping the event.

She told him, "I don't care. I'm going."

Even when the running became difficult, she wasn't discouraged.

"Whatever pain I had during the race, it's really nothing compared to what other people have experienced," she said.

Indeed, a special moment for Wyllie was when she passed the Terry Fox statue in downtown Ottawa.

"Talk about an inspiring moment," she says. "I still remember that very clearly. It made me a little weepy."

Her other lasting memory from the race is the fact that the volunteers were waiting for her more than six hours after the start of the race.

"It was so wonderful that they were there at the end," she says. "I didn't think they would wait that long. Hats off to them. They really cared about the people that were running."

As she approached the finish, two of Wyllie's Nortel teammates who had already crossed came back to run the final few hundred metres alongside her. But they let her cross the finish line all by herself.

"An organizer said to me, 'They always remember who was first and who was last,'" she says. "I said, 'Fantastic.'"

After the race, Wyllie says the group piled into a car and drove for five hours back to the Toronto area.

"I remember it wasn't easy trying to get out of the van after all that running and driving," she says.

Looking back 25 years later, Wyllie says the important thing is not that she finished last, but that she finished.

"It was very difficult and somewhat painful, but that didn't really matter in the end," she says. "It was an amazing experience, a close second to having my son. Every time I talk about it, I smile."

Although she kept running for several years, Wyllie never entered another marathon.

"That was my first and my last," she says. "And I don't care how long it took me. I did it, and it was a huge accomplishment for me."

"I don't care how long it took me. I did it, and it was a huge accomplishment for me."

DEBBIE WYLLIE

SIBLING RIVALRY

Jack Callaci (bib number 7) of Rhode Island wasn't just focused on finishing the race. He says he was thinking about his younger brother Chris, who was running ahead of him. "The worst part was that I was always close enough to see him and think that I could catch him. I still remember those bright yellow shorts he wore," remembers Callaci. "Chris was living with me then and we trained together. My wife didn't appreciate our Sunday workout – 15 miles in the morning, a nap, and 15 miles in the afternoon." The brothers came to Ottawa with their friend Larry Cassassa, who planned to run the 10k. "We persuaded him to run the marathon instead on the logic that the marathon was easier than a 10k because it was less intense. The poor guy took our advice. After we finished the marathon and were recovered, we waited for our friend. As he approached the finish line, he had that totally washed-out, empty look. Chris and I felt very guilty. Lucky for us, he is still a good friend."

WHEELCHAIR HEROES

Andre Beaudoin won the men's wheelchair marathon, and British athlete Josie Cichockyj won the women's race. Only a month after winning in Ottawa, Cichockyj went on to win the London Marathon. Cichockyj has set 28 British track records, from 100m through to 5,000m. She gave up marathons in 1989 to play for Great Britain's Wheelchair Basketball team, serving as the team captain from 1989 to 1992 and competing in the 1988 Paralympics in Seoul, South Korea and the 1996 Paralympics in Atlanta.

1989

MOTHER'S DAY BONUS

Lise Bouchard of Cap-Rouge, Quebec celebrated Mother's Day by running a personal best, winning the women's division by almost six minutes. Her Mother's Day gift was a prize of $3,600. "It's my biggest cheque by far," she told the *Ottawa Citizen*. Bouchard had competed in the 1984 Ottawa Marathon, but had taken a four-year break from competitive running to raise her son.

INTRODUCING THE LOONIE

Canadian wallets became a lot heavier. The one-dollar bill was replaced by the dollar coin.

FEDERAL FIRST

Audrey McLaughlin was elected leader of the New Democratic Party, replacing Ed Broadbent and becoming the first woman to lead a Canadian federal political party.

LEARNING TO LEAD

Defending champion **Gord Christie** took home the top prize once again in 1989, shaving almost four minutes off his time from the year before. By the 15-kilometre mark, Christie was well ahead of the rest of the pack and had to run the race mostly on his own. "I'm never a great frontrunner. I definitely prefer to run with someone. But it showed me I am a lot stronger than I thought," he told the *Ottawa Citizen* after the race.

THIRD AND BEST

Andy Jones finished third in a time of 2:19:25, his best result at the Ottawa Marathon. He ran his first Ottawa Marathon in 1983. "In the early 80s, it was a novelty," he said. "Everyone was going to go out and run a marathon. Well, everybody's run his one marathon."

1,285
marathon participants

🌡 **+14c**

2:18:38
Gord Christie
Men's Winner

2:49:33
France Levasseur
Women's Winner

3,000
Race Weekend participants

Hooked on marathons

How many marathons has Wally Herman completed?

"Let me see," he says, thumbing through his notebook. "Seven hundred and twenty-eight."

Herman started recording all of his races when he had finished 100 marathons. He writes the date, the location and a few notes about the weather and how the race went.

"I'm only doing two or three a year now," he quickly adds. Only. Wally Herman is 88 years old.

And how many times has he finished the Ottawa Marathon? "I don't know, maybe 20, max. I'll have to count them up and let you know." He calls back the next day. "I'm surprised," he says. "Of the 39, gosh, I've participated in 33 of them."

He didn't run the first Ottawa Marathon because in May 1975, Wally Herman wasn't running marathons. His first came in October of that year, in Kitchener-Waterloo. So the 728 marathons have happened over the course of 39 years, an average of about 19 a year. And every single one of them after Herman turned 49.

Herman was born in Winnipeg and moved to Ottawa for a job in the federal public service. He did some cross-country skiing and enjoyed long walks, but didn't have an interest in running until he watched American Frank Shorter win the 1972 Olympic Marathon in Munich.

"That sparked my interest," he says. Shorter's win is often credited for launching a running boom in North America. But few people who took up long-distance running embraced it as fully as Herman.

"The first one I thought, 'I'll do one and that's it, I'll get it out of my system,'" he said a few years ago. "But then you're hooked."

After his debut in the fall of 1975, Herman ran seven in 1976, including the second edition of the Ottawa Marathon. He ran 15 in 1977, 17 in 1978, and 19 in 1979. In each of the 20 years after that, he ran at least 20 marathons.

"I took an early retirement," he says. "That's what made it possible for me. I had the time."

Herman started travelling North America by bus, buying 10-day Greyhound passes so he could run a marathon in one city one weekend and another the next. Along the way, he became the first person to run a marathon in all 50 U.S. states. He completed marathons in 12 Canadian provinces and territories, then added Nunavut when it was created in 1999.

He's also travelled the world, finishing marathons in 99 different countries. He was the first to tick off all seven continents, including Antarctica. If you leave out all of his training and just add up the kilometres from his marathons, he's run more than 30,000 kilometres, three-quarters of the distance around the world.

Ottawa, he says, stands up well against many of the marathons he's experienced.

"It's one of the nicer ones," he says, "because of the great route and the good organization."

And he doesn't always stop at 42.2 kilometres. Herman has completed 70 races of 50k or longer.

"They're all a blend of pain and pleasure," he says. "I always look forward to the next one. It's so good to get out there amongst all those great people who have decided that this is a good thing to do.

"It's exercise and it's good for you. And you meet some great people. I never met a horse's ass in all those people."

He doesn't run much anymore, but Herman walks and swims daily and plans to finish three marathons in 2014, including Ottawa.

"It's been a great ride for me," he says. "Oh my gosh. Going to 99 countries really leaves something with you."

"Of the 39,
gosh, I've
participated
in 33
of them."

WALLY HERMAN

A LITTLE HELP FROM FRIENDS

The women's winner, **France Levasseur**, stirred up controversy by being paced to the finish line. For most of the race, the 32-year-old from Quebec City ran on the heels of two of her male training partners who provided her with instructions and shelter from the wind. Other runners, including 1989 champion Lise Bouchard, complained to race organziers. But despite an official protest, an appeals committee determined Levasseur did not break the rules because she was not physically assisted.

FIRST STEP

Robyn Dicesare of Winnipeg still has the shoes she wore for her first Ottawa Marathon. "They represent the beginning of my marathon journey," she says. "I'm at 38 marathons and counting, including 10 Boston Marathons." She says she was "hooked" right from the start.

BIG NUMBERS

Runners drank 140,000 cups of water and 80,000 cups of Coca-Cola and consumed fifty watermelons and 60 cases of other fruit (about 3,000 apples, oranges and bananas) during and after the race. A total of 1,200 volunteers helped out, including a medical staff of 140.

BACK IN TIME

The novel Jurassic Park by Michael Crichton was published.

TRIPLE CROWN

Gord Christie won the marathon for the third consecutive year.

FIRST OF MANY

Twenty-year-old **David Giroux** (bib 1404) ran his first Ottawa Marathon in 2:53:11. He has since participated in either the marathon or the half-marathon 15 times. In 2012, his three daughters entered the kids' marathon. Giroux says he plans "to race Ottawa until I can't walk anymore."

DAWN OF A NEW ERA

In the fall of 1990, Tim Berners-Lee created the first web server and thus the foundation for the World Wide Web; it would be released to the public in 1991.

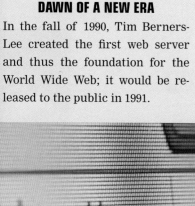

1990 OTTAWA

HEALTHY RUN

Ottawa-Carleton's medical officer of health **Stephen Corber** finished his second and last marathon. "For a while I felt younger, but now I'm feeling older," he told the *Ottawa Citizen*. Looking back many years later, he remembered that it was cloudy and cool at the starting line. "I was wondering whether I should dress more warmly," he says. "In fact, I was comfortable within a few minutes and felt easy all the way, almost carried along; the crowds along the side of the route helped too. I finished with a better time than I could have imagined and never tried another marathon."

1990

UPSET WIN

Led by **Bob Rae,** the Ontario NDP won the 1990 election to form their first government in the province.

BEST OF MANY

For **Joe Du Vall** (bib 4123), who ran Ottawa in 16 of the 17 years between 1979 and 1995, the 1990 marathon was the best marathon he'd ever run, although his fastest time was 2:52:45 in 1981. "It was the best marathon I've ever run," he says. Breaking three hours, Du Vall adds, is "tough to do. Everything has to be right." A fixture on the Ottawa running scene for more than 35 years, Du Vall has been a volunteer and race director for many events. He was hired on a three-month contract to help with Ottawa Race Weekend operations in 2006 and eventually became a full-time employee of the event in 2007.

1994 OTTAWA

LAST BUT NOT LEAST

Race organizers brought out the tape not just for the first runner to cross the finish line, but also the last. **Malcolm Niblett** was running his first marathon at age 60 after having a silent heart attack four years earlier on a training run. "I just thought I'll never be 60 again, so I thought it would be good to run a marathon," Niblett told the *Ottawa Citizen*. He combined running and walking to finish the race in 6:11:14. Niblett also received a special medal engraved with the words "Last finisher."

PRECIOUS MEDALS

Michel Villeneuve of St. Jerome, Quebec, ran his first marathon in 1990. He went on to accumulate a collection of medals over the years, completing 20 Ottawa Marathons.

1991

From "never again" to every spring

1,600
marathon participants

🌡 **+24c**

2:23:44
Michael Petrocci
Men's Winner

2:51:00
Laura Konantz
Women's Winner

5,100
Race Weekend participants

For David McClintock, the Ottawa Marathon has become an annual routine, a fixture in his schedule since 1985.

"I'm a creature of habit," he says. "And every May, it's the marathon. It's in my calendar from the start of the year."

In 1984, the last year he didn't run the Ottawa Marathon, McClintock was an elite water polo player who just missed making Canada's Olympic team. When he realized that his career in the pool was coming to an end, he decided to take up triathlons.

"I knew the writing was on the wall, so I went down to the bike store and got myself a bike," he says. "I started to think about doing some races. I quickly realized I should be a good runner to compete in triathlons. So I signed up for a marathon in Toronto."

McClintock says he didn't thoroughly prepare for his first marathon, relying mostly on the conditioning he had from his water polo training. He finished the race in a good time, but was completely exhausted when it was over.

"I remember saying to someone, 'Never again,'" he says.

But he quickly abandoned that promise to himself. Within a few weeks, he says, he was planning to run Ottawa in 1985.

"I guess we humans forget the pain and start thinking about doing better. I got bitten with the bug and I started thinking it wasn't that bad after all. I guess I forgot half the stuff that happened."

It was the beginning of a streak that is now approaching 30 years. Since 1985, he has run Ottawa every May without fail.

Along the way, he's also completed many triathlons, including Ironman events. Like many multisport athletes, he uses the Ottawa Marathon as an annual fitness test, a race that is perfectly timed to inspire hard training from January through May, with race day arriving just before triathlon season gets into full swing.

"I look forward to it every year," he says. "It reassures me that I'm still fairly fit. It's a checkpoint every year to say that I'm still there and I can do it. I really enjoy that sort of measure for myself.

"It's the start of summer, and I always know if I can do well in the marathon, then I'm set for a good season."

But there is also something about the consistency of running the Ottawa Marathon every May that appeals to him.

"Once I start doing something, I want to continue doing it and see how many I can do," he says. "After I'd done about 10 or 15 I realized this was something I was going to be doing every year for as long as I could."

McClintock says he thought his streak was significant until he started running the Boston Marathon every year.

"I met a bunch of people in Boston that make a streak of 30 years look like nothing," he says. "I remember passing one guy who was doing his 150th marathon and his 50th or 60th in Boston. I got humbled very quickly."

And of course, there are the three runners who have run Ottawa every single year since it began. They may have 10 marathons on him, but McClintock has them in his sights.

"I said to myself six or seven years ago, one day I'd like to be the one that's done the most consecutive Ottawa Marathons," he says.

"Outside of family events, the two things I look forward to most every year are Boston and Ottawa. Those are the two events of my life that I will continue to do as long as I can do them.

"And I plan to do them for an awfully long time."

"After I'd done about 10 or 15, I realized this was something I was going to be doing every year for as long as I could."

DAVE McCLINTOCK

MIXED MOTHER'S DAY

Michael Petrocci won his first of back-to-back Ottawa Marathon titles. The physician from St. Catharines, Ontario says he has many fond memories of Ottawa and that the race was always perfectly timed for his training. But because it used to fall on Mother's Day, it required a compromise from his wife. "It always led to a rather disappointing Mother's Day for Valerie," he jokes. "She often ended up having her supper on the way home, at the Swiss Chalet in Belleville.'"

CHEERS FROM THE HILL

Ron Merkley remembers vividly the moments before his first marathon in 1991. "What an experience," he says. "I can still remember standing at the starting line in '91, filled with anticipation, waiting for the starting gun to go off. All of a sudden the gun goes off – and no one moves. In the distance, I can see heads starting to bob and run above the crowd. Slowly, the bobbing gets closer and closer until finally we are able to run; what a rush." Merkley says he enjoyed being able to run past the Parliament Buildings. "As I approached Parliament, there was an enormous crowd on the Hill, cheering on everyone who ran by. Because of their support, I was able to continue without stopping."

1991

SURVIVING THE HEAT

Laura Konantz may have finished 10 minutes slower than her personal best, but it was good enough to win her the women's title. Running in warm temperatures, Konantz took the lead after about 30 kilometres, passing Helene Blais and Sylviane Puntous. "I was very fit and ready to compete with anybody. The marathon was on Mother's Day and we woke up to a freak heat wave in May. It was hot! After training in the cool spring weather, this was quite a shock to everyone," she remembers. "I could see Sylvaine struggling as well, and at about 34k I passed her. By this time, the sun was hot, and I kept pouring water over my head. I could see the finish line and stumbled across." Konantz's time was 2:51. She earned a trip to Cuba for the Pan Am Games.

PAIN AND GAIN

27-year-old Steve Welchner may not have been the fastest runner on the course, finishing in just under five hours, but he did meet his goal: raising $8,000 for Ottawa's Shepherds of Good Hope. Welchner started training in January, but made the mistake of overtraining. And he paid for it. By the time the Ottawa lawyer showed up at the starting line of his first marathon he required supportive devices on both knees, and orthotic inserts in his shoes. "I have a vivid recollection of starting out the marathon with a brace on each of my knees, wondering how I was possibly going to finish. It was the first time I prayed, and then felt no knee pain for the whole race. The pain didn't come back until the following day," he remembers. It was Welchner's first and last marathon. "My knees never recovered enough to run long distances."

SCARY MOVIE

Hannibal Lecter made moviegoers think differently about "a nice Chianti," and *Silence Of The Lambs* won the big five at the Oscars: Best Picture, Best Director, Best Actor, Best Actress, and Best Writing.

EARLY START

Octogenarians Mavis Lindgren of California and Charles Benovoy of Ottawa were given an early start to the marathon. Both began the race 75 minutes ahead of the rest of the runners. Lindgren was 84 at the time, and Benovoy 80.

CELEBRATING IN STYLE

When Ottawa's **Tony Fletcher** crossed the finish line of the Ottawa marathon for his seventh time, it was his third major accomplishment in less than six months. To celebrate his 40th birthday, Fletcher ran the New York City Marathon in November 1990, climbed Argentina's Mount Aconcagua in January, and completed the 17th Ottawa Marathon. "You only turn 40 once and you're only young once," the voice actor and announcer told the *Ottawa Citizen*.

GULF WAR I

Canadian forces joined the multinational forces in the battle to drive Saddam Hussein's Iraqi troops from Kuwait.

SHOCKING RETIREMENT

Magic Johnson announced he was ending his career with the L.A. Lakers after having contracted HIV.

1992

A rich father-son experience

1,259
marathon participants

🌡+23c

2:20:03
Michael Petrocci
Men's Winner

2:47:55
Betsy Kneale
Women's Winner

4,502
Race Weekend participants

When Chris Berzins was in his final year of high school, teachers across the school board went on strike. As the dispute stretched on for almost a month, Berzins did two things to fill in the extra time: he took a job as an overnight security guard, and he started training for the Ottawa Marathon.

Berzins' father Andrejs, a high-profile Crown attorney in Ottawa, had already run the marathon a couple of times. So father and son started training together, running early in the morning when Chris got home from work and sharing long runs on the weekend.

"It was a great way to spend time together," says Chris, who now works at the Canadian embassy in Washington.

And it followed something of a pattern. When Chris was in his early teenage years, he and Andrejs completed a ski marathon in Gatineau together a few times. They also biked the Rideau Lakes Cycle Tour. So training together for a long-distance run wasn't a giant leap.

"Chris and I have always been very close, and like doing activities together," says Andrejs. "He was always interested in these kinds of things that I was doing. So he got into it. We started cycling together and skiing together. And then we both thought it would be neat if we did a marathon together."

Andrejs was a successful athlete in university, competing in wrestling and playing on the McGill Redmen football team. But running did not come naturally to him.

"I was never a good runner," he says. "As a matter of fact, I was always a terrible runner."

But when he started his legal career, he devoted more time to work and less to sports and decided he needed to do something to maintain his fitness.

"I started getting out of shape," he says. "There were a couple of people in my office who were training for the marathon, and I envied these guys going running at lunch hour. So I decided I would see if I could do it myself."

From there, he got into cycling and skiing, and inspired his son to do the same. Chris says he wasn't as good an athlete as his father was in high school. He rode the bench on the football team, he says, because he wasn't very big or very fast. But he discovered he had some endurance, so a marathon was an appropriate challenge.

So every weekend, the Berzins would set off for their long training run.

"It was neat, as you kind of built the clock up together, starting at a 10-miler and working your way up to three hours," says Chris. "We would chat about whatever, tell jokes, and plan our water stops. It was great."

"I wish I could say they were profound discussions, but there really weren't," says Andrejs. "It was just an opportunity to spend time together and have the same goals."

And it's an activity they have continued to share ever since. The Berzins have never entered another marathon together – the 1992 race was the last for Andrejs, while Chris ran another almost 20 years later – but they have continued to run together. As Chris's education and career have taken him to destinations all over the world, he and Andrejs have headed out for a run whenever they've been in the same city.

"If we get together, one of the first things we do is go for a run," says Andrejs.

"In my time overseas, he's run with me in Hyde Park in London," says Chris. "When I was in Prague, he would run with me. In Brussels, in Riga in Latvia, where I lived for a year. And here in Washington."

On race day in 1992, the Berzins ran together for the first half of the race, then Andrejs let his son go ahead without him. They finished about half an hour apart, then went to get an ice cream together.

"It was a really rich experience," says Andrejs. "It was an opportunity to do something with my son that we both enjoyed. We got a lot out of it."

"It was an opportunity to do something with my son that we both enjoyed."

ANDREJS BERZINS

LONELY FINISH

Betsy Kneale of Syracuse, New York, missed beating Chris Lavallee's 1978 Ottawa marathon course record by just 17 seconds. "I knew I was under 2:51 (coming down the finish line)," she told the *Ottawa Citizen*. "I wanted to beat it." Kneale says she was "a little lonely" during the race, running on her own for much it. Her closest competitor, Ottawa triathlete Laura Ruptash, crossed the finish line almost 15 minutes later. It was Ruptash's first marathon. Audrey Fyke of Kincardine, Ontario finished third in 3:06:03

TRAILBLAZER
On board the shuttle Discovery, **Roberta Bondar** became Canada's first female astronaut.

NOT SO LITTLE

Diana King, of Carleton Place, Ontario was the 14th woman to cross the finish line, in 3:29:27. But it isn't just the finish she remembers. "At the start in the Carleton University parking lot, my friend Colleen and I encountered a group of five very fit, muscular male colleagues of her husband. Her husband was on the RCMP special task force at the time. They teased us about what we 'little women' were doing in such a long, tough race and did we think we could finish it. Even at that time, there were significantly more men running the NCM than women. Colleen and I left them behind in our dust after 15 km. Very satisfying."

LOTS OF FUEL

Race organizers trucked in 7,800 bottles of Evian water, 1,200 cans of low-alcohol beer, 3,000 containers of yogurt, and 1,500 bananas and oranges to feed the runners. The race's medical team treated 143 runners, mostly for blisters, sprains, and cramps.

JUST OUT FOR A STROLL

Bernard Cote didn't just get himself across the finish line in an impressive 3:34, he brought his son Gabriel along with him. For the second year in a row, Cote pushed a stroller containing his three-year-old boy. "We just have fun," Bernard told the *Ottawa Citizen*. "We sing during the run. We spend lots of time talking." Both father and son received finishing medals for their teamwork.

MAVIS DOES IT AGAIN

Mavis Lindgren, 85, of Orleans, California got an early start to the marathon again this year. "Marvellous Mavis," the race's oldest runner, began her race at 7:15 to beat the heat, completing the course in 7:09:47. It was Lindgren's 61st marathon since turning 70.

ANOTHER SUMMIT REACHED

53-year-old Vladimir Nadbakh of Moscow, was 13th overall and an easy winner in his age category with a time of 2:43:36. The former Russian mountain climbing champion wanted to break 2:40 just 20 days after running 2:40:15 at the Boston Marathon. "It wasn't enough rest after Boston," Nadbakh told the *Ottawa Citizen*'s Wayne Scanlan. "At 10k, I could feel my legs were not light."

1992

A FEW MORE LEFT TO GO

Bruce Barteaux finished in two hours and 51 minutes. "I want to run one under 2:40, that's my goal. I keep saying I'm not getting older, I'm getting faster. But the last two years, I have gone slower," he told the *Ottawa Citizen*. "I believe I still have a few more marathons left in me. Maybe some of us are just too stupid to quit doing them." Barteaux definitely had a few more marathons in him. More than 20 years later, Barteaux is still running. He's finished 73 marathons, missing only a handful in Ottawa since running his first in 1980. "I still run about one marathon a year, which is usually the Ottawa one."

NEW KIDS IN TOWN

The **Ottawa Senators** returned to the NHL after a 58-year hiatus. The Senators won their first game of the regular season against the Montreal Canadiens, but won only nine other games the rest of the year, setting three NHL records that season: longest home losing streak, longest road losing streak, and the fewest road wins in a season – one.

SPECIAL DAY FOR DAD

Harry Welten cooled off by dumping some water over his head. Running with him is Malcolm Gains (#5058). Welten ended up placing fourth overall. But that wasn't the most exciting part of his day. Two days before the marathon, his second daughter was born. As soon as the race was over, he headed straight to the hospital to pick up his wife and newborn daughter to bring them home. "A memorable weekend for sure," he says.

BIG COMEBACK

Just 10 weeks after breaking her leg in a rowing accident, **Silken Laumann** won the Olympic bronze medal in single sculls.

BEST BOOK

The English Patient, by Michael Ondaatje, won the Booker Prize and the Governor General's Award.

1993

965
marathon participants

🌡+25c

2:23:14
Jean Lagarde
Men's Winner

2:52:31
Noeleen Wadden
Women's Winner

4,215
Race Weekend participants

Out of nowhere

The only person to have won the Ottawa Marathon four years in a row came from relative obscurity and soon disappeared right back into it.

Three days before he won the 1993 marathon, Jean Lagarde wasn't even planning to run the race. At the time, Lagarde was a 29-year-old phys-ed student living in Montreal. Just days before the race, he was visiting the home of a fellow Montrealer, a bus driver named Tom Marathakis.

"I was going to go to Ottawa and run the 10k race just for the fun of it," says Marathakis. "I said, 'Johnny, what are you doing tomorrow?' I wanted him to come along."

According to Marathakis, Lagarde told him he planned to do a long run that weekend. "I said, 'Why don't you come to Ottawa and watch me run? Then on the Sunday morning you can do your run during the marathon.'"

Lagarde and Marathakis drove to Ottawa on Saturday. Marathakis ran the 10k, and Lagarde registered for the marathon at 4:30 p.m., just hours before the race the following morning.

The next day was probably the hottest in the history of the event, with temperatures hitting as high as 28 degrees. Lagarde won by a huge margin, four minutes ahead of any other runner.

"I decided to run the National Capital for a long run," Lagarde told *Ottawa Citizen* in 1993. "I was alone after eight kilometres, and I felt I could win."

Wayne Scanlan wrote in the *Citizen* that the margin of victory was so large, a brass band playing for the runners had time for an intermission between Lagarde and the next runner.

He may have done the race on a whim, but Lagarde wasn't inexperienced at distance running. Marathakis says his friend trained regularly and was a gifted runner. Lagarde told reporters that he ran 35k every Sunday, doing seven five-kilometre laps of Montreal's Maisonneuve Park.

The next year, Lagarde had an even lonelier race. He finished six minutes ahead of the field in a marathon that was characterized by the *Citizen* as "ho-hum." The *Citizen*'s Martin Cleary wrote that Lagarde looked almost bored when he crossed the finish line. Scanlan described him as "laconic."

"I was alone and many minutes ahead," Lagarde told the media. "After 30 kilometres, I knew I'd won."

In 1995, Lagarde, now described as a night-shift bellhop from Saint-Sauveur, Quebec, was recovering from injuries and running his first race since the previous Ottawa Marathon. He overcame stomach cramps to prevail with the slowest winning time in the history of the race.

In 1996, three years after prevailing in 28-degree heat, Lagarde won the race in snow squalls and windchills of minus-8. Despite the cold, Lagarde ran without a hat or gloves, and even wore silk shorts, according to Cleary's report in the *Citizen*.

Lagarde returned in 1997 to attempt a fifth consecutive win. But he began to suffer leg cramps 17 kilometres into the race and, although he remained with the leaders until just past the halfway point, he dropped out at 28 kilometres.

And he's barely been heard of since. Marathakis says Lagarde still lives in Saint-Sauveur and, while he continues to run regularly, he no longer competes in races.

Marathakis is one of the few people from Lagarde's winning days in Ottawa who is still in touch with him.

"Johnny is a very simple, soft-spoken guy," says Marathakis. "A super nice guy, very straightforward. But a very private, introverted person."

Were it not for the last-minute invitation from Marathakis, Lagarde may never have run Ottawa. Instead, he remains one of only two four-time men's champions, and the only man to win four consecutive Ottawa Marathons.

> "I was alone and many minutes ahead. After 30 kilometres, I knew I'd won."
>
> **JEAN LAGARDE**

:13.11

FIVE-TIME PARALYMPIAN

Legendary paralympian **André Viger** won the wheelchair race in a course record time. Viger captured his first Ottawa marathon win in 1:40:13, beating Luke Gingras's record of 1:45:20. Between 1980 and 1996 Viger competed at five Paralympic Games, winning three gold medals, four silver, and three bronze. He became the first Canadian to win a medal at a Paralympic demonstration event when he won bronze in the 1,500 metres at the Los Angeles Olympics in 1984. Viger won the men's wheelchair division of the Boston Marathon in 1984, 1986, and 1987. Viger died of cancer on October 1, 2006, at the age of 54.

APPLAUDED LIKE A CHAMP

In a letter to the *Ottawa Citizen*, **Dr. L.P. Schnurr** of Morrisburg, Ontario wrote, "This past Sunday, for the first time ever, I competed in a marathon, completing the National Capital Marathon in four hours plus. While my time is nothing to brag about, the quality of the event itself deserves loud praise...My name called aloud as I stumbled across the finish line, applauded by all as though I were a champ, then solicitously cooled off and led to refreshments. What an Olympian effort these kind people produced."

I WANT TO BELIEVE

The *X-Files* television series, created by Chris Carter, aired for the first time. The show ran from September 10, 1993 to May 19, 2002, spanning nine seasons and 202 episodes.

FLOWERS AT THE FINISH

Colleen Patterson (left) and **Suzanne Bailey** each received a Mother's Day rose at the finish line.

WHEN THE WHEELS FELL OFF

Andy Shelp ran his first ever marathon. He and his wife, Tanis, were passionate about triathlons when Shelp decided it might be "interesting" to try a marathon before he turned 30. His first race didn't go exactly as planned, but it didn't stop him from running more marathons in the future. "The first half of my race went great," he says, "then the wheels fell off, as is often the case, right around the 20-mile mark. My time for the first half of the race: 1:25. Overall time: 3:52. I would say that the Ottawa marathon changed our lives forever. We went on to do many more marathons over the following years."

JAYS REPEAT

The **Toronto Blue Jays** won the World Series for the second year in a row.

SPOT THE DOG

Ty Warner USA launched *Beanie Babies*.

FROM THE ROCK

After not being able to complete the 1991 Ottawa Marathon, **Noeleen Wadden** of St. John's, Newfoundland, won the women's title in 1993. She went on to win the marathon again in 1995. Twenty years later, Wadden has fond memories of the race. "There were many people along the course, even some fellow Newfoundlanders, who called-out very encouraging words as I ran past," she says. "The 1993 marathon was my first marathon victory, and it was an exhilarating feeling to cross the finish line, as there were many people gathered at the finish."

BANNED BEN

Disgraced Canadian sprinter **Ben Johnson** was banned from athletics for life.

1993

MAKING HISTORY

Kim Campbell replaced Brian Mulroney as the leader of the Progressive Conservative party, becoming Canada's first female prime minister. Campbell was defeated by Liberal Jean Chrétien in the 35th general election. After being in power for nine years, the Conservatives were reduced to two seats in the House of Commons.

TORTUROUS DAY

Cheered on by her family, **Nancy Morrison** of Kanata celebrated Mother's Day by placing second in 2:58:48. "What a way to spend Mother's Day, torturing yourself," she told the *Ottawa Citizen*.

1994

MAY

8

866

marathon participants

❄+14c

2:19:00

Jean Lagarde

Men's Winner

2:50:52

France Levasseur

Women's Winner

3,504

Race Weekend participants

Marvelous Mavis

As she crossed the finish line of her fourth Ottawa Marathon in 1994, 87-year-old great-grandmother Mavis Lindgren was greeted by honking horns and a bouquet of roses.

"I don't know how it could have been any nicer," Lindgren told the *Citizen* after the race

"I do have sore feet," she added. "But that's nothing against the marathon."

Lindgren went on to say how glad she was to be an example of good health principles. "It's fantastic what can be accomplished," she said.

In Lindgren's case, it's nothing short of amazing.

Born in Manitoba in 1907, Lindgren entered a 50-yard dash at a church picnic when she was 10 years old. That was her last race for more than half-a-century.

Lindgren was often sick in her childhood. She had whooping cough when she was two, tuberculosis at 13. Even as an adult, her health faltered frequently. Colds often turned into something worse, including bronchitis. She suffered from pneumonia four times in a five year period in her late 50s.

"Seemed like if I got cold feet and they stayed cold for two hours, I was on my way to pneumonia," she told the *New York Times* in 1993.

That all changed when Lindgren was 62. She attended a seminar that recommended walking and jogging to improve overall health. She started going for brisk walks and runs, initially in her regular clothes. Drivers would stop and ask if she needed help, thinking she was running to or from something.

Her health, she later said, improved almost immediately. And seven years after she launched her new regimen, her son Kelvin surprised Lindgren by entering her in a 20-mile road race in California, where the family then lived.

At 69, she did so well in the race that Kelvin signed her up for her first marathon, which she ran just after turning 70. She must have enjoyed the experience, because by the time she turned

71, she'd finished four of them.

Over the next 21 years, she ran a total of 75 marathons, becoming an international phenomenon. *Runner's World* searched U.S. race records and couldn't find another woman over 70 who had ever run a marathon. *Sports Illustrated* wrote an article about her in 1978. When she turned 80, researchers at a university in California tested Lindgren and determined she had the fitness level of an average woman between the ages of 22 and 29.

She ran the Ottawa for the first time in 1991, at the age of 84. After it was over, she gushed about the race. "It was a beautiful marathon," she told the *Citizen*. "I've never run a more beautiful marathon." And at that point, she'd run 58 of them.

She earned a reputation as an unstoppable force, running in hot and cold temperatures, through pouring rain, and even finishing a marathon after falling and breaking her wrist – when she was 85 years old. She completed the London Marathon on her 88th birthday, with spectators singing 'Happy Birthday' to her along the course.

Lindgren didn't retire from running until she was 91. She passed away in 2001 at the age of 94, having inspired thousands of others with her energy and good nature and her message about healthy living.

"It just goes to show what a good lifestyle will do for you," she told the *Citizen* in 1993, after her third of four consecutive Ottawa Marathons.

In 1993 she was accompanied along the course by a group of high school students who had raised the funds to pay for her trip to Ottawa.

"It couldn't have been a more beautiful day," she said after the race. "I had nice, warm, caring, and friendly people with me."

The affection Lindgren had for Ottawa was always mutual. At the finish line of her first Ottawa Marathon in 1991, Lindgren told the *Citizen*'s Martin Cleary, "I'm really enamoured with this beautiful city." Cleary wrote that a spectator then chimed in, "And it with you."

I've never run a more beautiful marathon.

MAVIS LINDREN

LONG WALK TO POWER

Nelson Mandela became South Africa's first black president after more than three centuries of white rule.

LOW EXPECTATIONS

When 1990 champ **France Levasseur** of Ste-Foy, Quebec started the 1994 marathon, she wasn't sure she would even complete it. "My goal was to do a training run for 30 km," she told the *Ottawa Citizen*. "If I had good time and was in a good position, I'd keep going." She kept going and won the women's race for the second time. Levasseur finished more than seven minutes ahead of defending champion Noeleen Wadden, who finished in 2:50:52. Nancy Morrison of Kanata was third in 3:04:32.

GOLD AND SILVER

Canadian men's champion **Elvis Stojko** won the 1994 World Championship and an Olympic silver medal in figure skating.

THERE FOR YOU

The first episode of the sitcom *Friends* aired on September 22, 1994.

BIG FINISH

Steve Watkins of Deux Montagnes, Quebec had enough energy left to jump for joy as he crossed the finish line.

WELCOME TO OTTAWA

Maurice Evlyn-Bufton, **Jim Clarke**, **Mark Wiltshire**, **John Whitby** and **David Russell** celebrated the 300th anniversary of the Royal Gloucestershire Berkshire Wiltshire Regiment of England by running the Ottawa Marathon. Ottawa was the fourth of five marathons they entered over seven months to raise money for Kenyan children needing cataract operations.

NICE RECOVERY

Harry Welten of Embrun, Ontario considered stopping at the halfway point because he felt ill, but he ended up finishing second in 2:25:12. And this was only 20 days after setting a personal best in Boston.

BEEP, BEEP

"I struggled for the last few miles with a very painful blister on the ball of my foot, but managed to hold off a fellow from Newfoundland," remembers Calgary's **Kelvin Broad**, who overcame the pain to finish third in 2:25:51. "The funny part of the race was that heart rate monitors had just come onto the scene, and some fellow in the bunch was wearing one and had it set to beep when he reached a certain heart rate. After about a mile, the beeping started. Not much later, the fellow drifted off the bunch either because he thought he was running too fast, or he was embarrassed that he didn't know how to stop it beeping!"

1994

INCREDIBLE JOURNEY

Jo Wells of Burlington, Ontario used the Ottawa Marathon as training for her cross-Canada run. After undergoing back surgery when she was 31, Wells began walking as part of her recovery. But walking quickly turned into running, which was her passion until she passed away in June 2012 at the age of 61. Over a 30-year running career, she completed marathons and ultramarathons in Canada, the United States, Europe, and the former Soviet Union. In 1994, she fulfilled her dream of running across Canada, covering 7,250 kilometres in 111 days. Although Wells wasn't the first woman to accomplish the feat, she was the fastest.

NO DISC

AMERICAN EXPRESS NATIONAL CAPITAL MARATHON

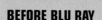

1994 OTTAWA

BEFORE BLU RAY

The first DVD player was created by Tatung Company in Taiwan in collaboration with Pacific Digital Company from the United States. The first players appeared in Japan in November, 1996, followed by U.S. players in March, 1997.

TOUCH THE SHOE!

After running the 1993 New York City Marathon, **Tom Lawson**, his wife Sheila, and a friend from Toronto named Andrew "Max" MacLeod went to a Russian art exhibit at the Guggenheim Museum. Something about seeing the exhibit right after the marathon tweaked MacLeod. "About two weeks later, this package arrives in the mail," says Tom Lawson. MacLeod had cut a shoe in half and nailed it to a board, painting asphalt below it and a sky above. "He called it 'Russian shoe.'" The Lawsons brought the piece of art with them when they watched the Ottawa Marathon the following year. "As people ran by, we would say 'Touch the shoe. It will give you good luck,'" says Lawson. Hundreds of people did. "Over the years this sort of crazy tradition has evolved around us," says Lawson.

1995

MAY
14

571
marathon participants

🌡+12c

2:26:53
Jean Lagarde
Men's Winner

2:58:51
Noeleen Wadden
Women's Winner

4,036
Race Weekend participants

Helping instead of running

Debby Whately has never run the Ottawa Marathon. But she's been on the course from start to finish every year for more than three decades.

In 1983, a friend with whom Whately played volleyball was training for the Ottawa Marathon. He asked if she wanted to run with him. She told him, "I don't run." But she agreed to ride a bike next to him on one of his training runs.

Then another friend told Whately she was helping to organize the area of the start and finish of the marathon. She asked for Whately's help.

"My girlfriend from high school wanted some help," she says. "I figured it would be a good thing to do, and I could see my friend who was running cross the finish line."

Every year since then, Whately has been one of the hundreds of volunteers who make the Ottawa Marathon possible for runners. She's usually on the course longer than any of the athletes, arriving early and staying until the final runner has crossed the finish line.

In her first few years as a volunteer, Whately helped to set up the start area, then prepared for when the runners returned.

"We had a very archaic way of recording who crossed the finish line," she says. In the days before computer chip timing, she and other volunteers would tear a portion of each runner's bib as he or she crossed the finish line and record it on a clipboard.

Over the years she has also served as a volunteer coordinator, and has set up and taken down the barricades that block the side streets where they intersect with the course.

Whately says the volunteers with whom she has worked are invariably dedicated and incredibly generous with their time.

"We start at 6:00 in the morning and we don't actually finish until the last runner is across the finish line," she says. "That could be 2:30 or 3:00 in the afternoon."

And the volunteers sometimes have a tough job. When she's worked the barricades, she's occasionally had to respond to drivers frustrated by the closed roads.

But she also hears from a lot of runners who appreciate the effort of the volunteers.

"Lots of them say thank you as they're going by," says Whately. "One fellow gave me a huge hug at the finish line while his girlfriend was saying, 'Who's the blonde?' But the hugs aren't the reason I do it."

Although she doesn't run, Whately participates in a number of other sports, including masters swimming and dragon-boat racing. She says that by giving her time to the Ottawa Marathon, she's passing on the benefit she receives from the people who support her events.

"I do other athletic activities that require volunteers," she says. "So this is my way of paying back the volunteers at my sports."

Whately also gets satisfaction from watching the thousands of athletes who have run past her over the years, including many of her friends.

"It's a lot of fun seeing all these runners," she says. "It's great to see the feeling of accomplishment. I know the satisfaction you get out of completing something. To be able to see that in the runners' faces gives me a little piece of satisfaction too."

Despite being inspired by all the runners she's witnessed, Whately has never been tempted to run the marathon instead of supporting it.

"It crossed my mind once or twice," she says. "But I'm not really into running. I'm an excellent swimmer. But I'm not a very good runner.

"I don't feel I'm doing nearly anything compared to the people running. But I enjoy being part of the whole weekend. This is my way of participating."

And her first experience as a volunteer, back in 1983, ended up being special for another reason.

"That friend of mine that ran it the first year eventually became my husband," she says.

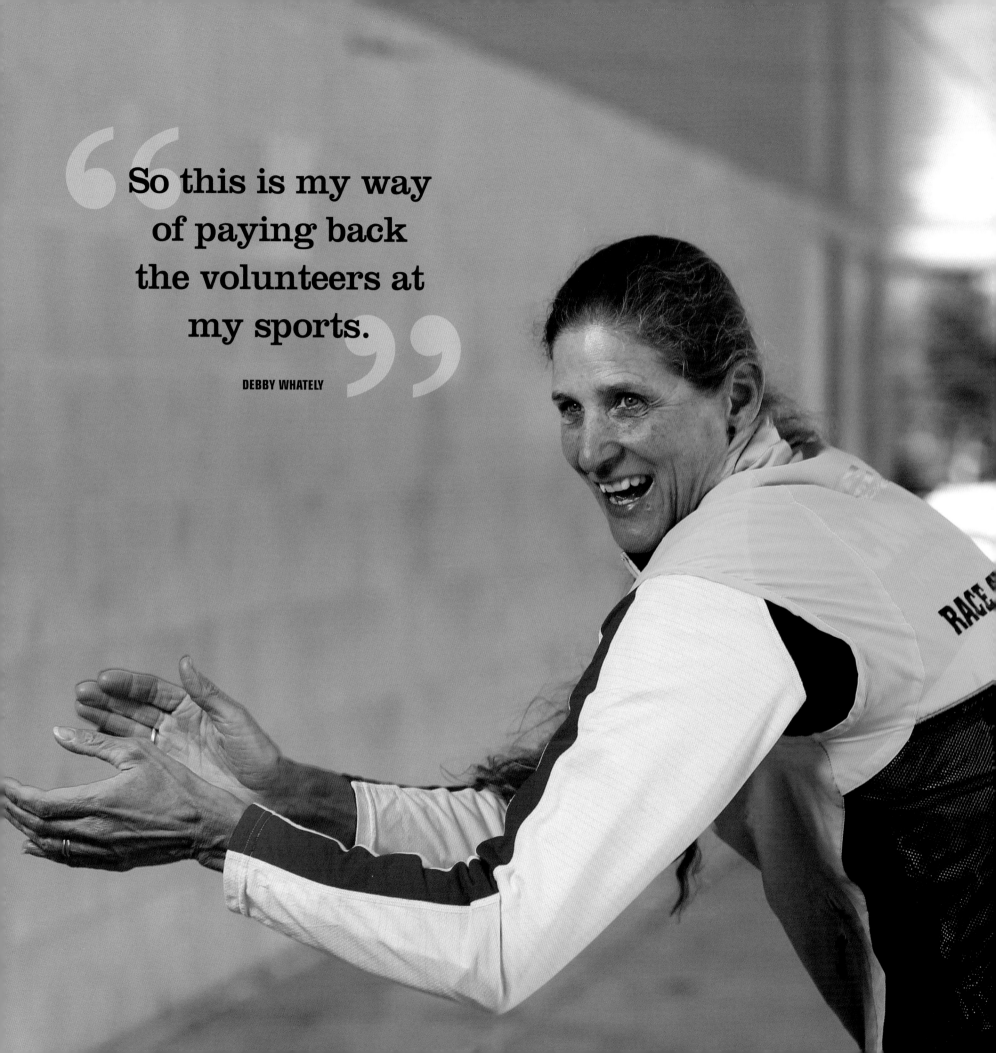

"So this is my way of paying back the volunteers at my sports."

DEBBY WHATELY

MARATHON MILESTONES

It was a year of firsts for the Ottawa Marathon. In-line skaters competed for the first time in an 8k race. The marathon's logo received a facelift, as the brand showing a male runner in front of the Peace Tower was replaced by a new logo showing several runners sprinting past the Peace Tower. The marathon course was also redeisgned. The out-and-back course starting at Carleton University and running along the parkway by the Ottawa River was replaced by a two-loop inner-city course through Hull and Ottawa. The marathon had no title sponsor, but was a sanctioned qualifying race for the 100th Boston Marathon in 1996.

GRATEFUL RUNNER

"I remember during the race, at every water station, there was always someone encouraging or telling me how far the next runner is; somehow, this motivated me to increase my speed and stay focused on the runner up ahead. Amongst the cheers, screams, and the friendly gestures, this gave me a boost of energy and [I] finished in a time of 2:31:04—fifth overall, and one of my best finishes at the marathon. Thank-you, Ottawa, for giving a Cree from Mistissini, Quebec region [a chance to] be part of your races in the 1990s."

Wally Rabbitskin

IS IT IRONIC?
Ottawa singer Alanis Morissette released *Jagged Little Pill*.

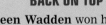

NO MORE MAVIS

Mavis Lindgren started the marathon for the fifth year in a row, but did not complete it. The 88-year-old dropped out at the 36-kilometre point after having fallen early in the r ace. Running 36 kilometres would be an amazing achievement for most great-grandmothers, but not for Lindgren. She was devastated that she didn't finish. It would be the last time that she made the trip to Ottawa. See her story in 1994.

NON, MERCI
By a narrow vote of 50.6 per cent to 49.4, sovereignty was rejected in the second Quebec Referendum.

VOTE
☐ Yes
☑ No

BACK ON TOP

Noeleen Wadden won her second women's title in three years in 2:58:51, the slowest winning time since 1977. Tina Kader finished just five seconds behind Wadden in her first race after taking a six-year break to have three children. Betsy Kneale of Syracuse, New York, the 1992 women's champion, places third in 3:00:47.

THE CHAMPION, AGAIN

Jean Lagarde of St-Sauveur, Quebec became the second man to win three consecutive Ottawa Marathons. It was his first race since winning the 1994 race, and it was definitely not his fastest time. At two hours, 26 minutes, 53 seconds, it was the slowest winning time in the marathon's 20-year history. Runner-up Alberto Dell'Appa of Toronto finished in 2:28:25 and David Ruggles of St. John's, Newfoundland placed third in 2:29:48.

1995

1996

MAY
12

805
marathon participants

🌡+1c

2:26:02
Jean Lagarde
Men's Winner

2:52:03
Kimberley Webb
Women's Winner

4,000
Race Weekend participants

The visionary

Not long after Jim Robinson took over management of the Ottawa Marathon in 1996, he set an audacious goal in an interview with Martin Cleary of the *Ottawa Citizen.*

"I'd like to see the marathon grow back to 1,500 to 2,000 runners," Robinson said.

It had been years since the marathon had been that popular. In 1996, the race had had barely 800 participants.

Robinson wasn't finished setting bold targets. He also told Cleary he expected Ottawa Race Weekend to grow to 10,000 participants by 2001.

Cleary, who had been covering the event for 20 years, politely described the objectives as "an ambitious vision," pointing out that the most successful Ottawa Race Weekend to date had been half that size.

"I'll never forget that first interview with Martin," says Robinson. "He did look at me like I was crazy."

Yet Robinson not only met, he exceeded his own expectations. In 2001, the event attracted 13,450 entrants, including more than 2,000 to the marathon.

And the growth didn't stop there. By the time Robinson stepped into semi-retirement in 2013, the event had exploded to more than 40,000 entrants, including more than 5,000 in the marathon.

Robinson had run the marathon himself during its first peak in popularity, finishing in just over three hours in 1979 and just under in 1980. He tried to break 2:50 in 1981, but started too fast and pulled out of the race after 32 kilometres.

In 1996, Robinson moved to Ottawa after retiring from 29 years in the Canadian military as a fitness, recreation, and sport officer. He decided to volunteer at the start area of the marathon. The general manager of the event announced he was planning to leave, and suggested Robinson apply for his job. Robinson was hired on a nine-month contract starting in the fall.

Robinson brought stability to an organization with a revolving door, leading the race for the next 17 years. For the first few editions, he was a one-man operation, working out of what he describes as a broom closet in the YMCA building, with just enough room for a desk and a filing cabinet.

He relied on volunteers and relatives to help with the operational details of the event. One year, his wife's grandmother put together all the safety pins that would be given to runners to attach their race bibs to their shirts.

Robinson oversaw a period of not only growth, but incredible change. In his first few years on the job, before online registration became popular, people mailed in their entries or dropped them at local stores. Most of the registrations arrived in the final few weeks. Robinson remembers walking to the bank by himself with $60,000 in cash.

"I remember thinking, 'What would happen if someone hit me over the head?'"

Robinson believed in the potential of the race because he felt Ottawa was a great place to run. One of his first moves was to start travelling to the race expos of marathons in other cities to promote Ottawa's event. He also established a race committee of volunteers who stayed involved from one year to the next so that the event wasn't starting over each time it was staged.

Robinson also attracted new investment from sponsors and government, reconnecting Ottawa Race Weekend with politicians and public sector officials who had stopped supporting the race. And he refocused on a priority set by the founders of the event: ensuring it was a good experience for runners.

"I knew that if you took care of the little things, the big things took care of themselves," he says. "It's the little things the runners want to be sure are looked after."

The results were so strong, it was hard to keep up. One year, last-minute registrations were so high that the race ran out of t-shirts.

"Ottawa is a special city," says Robinson. "All we had to do is get the word out there those first five or six years, because the organization of the event was top-notch. The word-of-mouth spread so fast, it was hard for us to keep up."

Since retiring from his full-time role in 2013, Robinson has continued to be involved in the event, working a few days a week to support the new leadership.

"It was a fantastic 17 years," he says. "To see where it came from and where it's at now. And I think it's only going to get better."

"I knew that if you took care of the little things, the big things took care of themselves."

JIM ROBINSON

LOST IN THE SNOW

About 15 minutes into the race, Jim Robinson remembers a young American man arriving at the start. "I explained the route to him and sent him on his way," says Robinson, pointing the man into what was almost a snowstorm. About 25 minutes later, Robinson saw the same man running toward him. "He had gotten lost," he says. "So I explained again how to make his way to the Alexandra Bridge, and this time he found his way and, believe it or not, he did both loops to complete the marathon. I am sure most of us, given the weather and getting lost for almost half hour, would have called it a day. Talk about tenacity. I would say he had it in spades."

BRRR...

The big story of the 1996 marathon was the weather. The runners raced through winter-like conditions: temperature of plus-one with a windchill of minus 8, north winds of 25 to 35 kilometres per hour, and light-to-heavy snow squalls. **Jean Lagarde** braved the elements without a hat or gloves and, according to media reports, donned silk shorts. He won his fourth straight Ottawa Marathon.

FASTEST MAN

Canadian **Donovan Bailey** won the 100-metre sprint at the Atlanta Summer Olympics in a new world-record time.

WEEKLY HABIT

For an entire year, from May 5, 1996 through April 27, 1997, **Karl Gruber**, of Hide-Away-Hills, Ohio ran a marathon a week. He called his effort to raise money for leukemia research the "Super Run for the Cure." Ottawa was the second marathon of his 52-week challenge, and he finished in 4:09:51. "The thing I remember about that race is that all of the pre-race material said, 'Come run during the Tulip Festival in Ottawa in May!' I'm thinking, 'Well, it's gonna be warm since the tulips will be blooming.' Ha ha!" Gruber says he loved Ottawa despite the chilly weather. "Such a beautiful, peaceful country, and Terry Fox is my personal hero. Ottawa really opened its arms to me."

1996

FATHER AND DAUGHTER

Chantal Desjardins remembers the 1996 marathon fondly, despite the cold weather. It was her first marathon. "Yes, it was memorable because it started snowing," she says. "However, this marathon is extremely special to me because on that day I realized a dream I've had growing up – running a marathon with my dad." Desjardins' father ran 53 marathons and three ultra-marathons throughout Canada and the States. In Ottawa, he ran side-by-side with his daughter as the rest of the family cheered them on. "It finished with a big hug that I will never forget," says Desjardins.

HONOURING HER BIGGEST FAN

Kimberley Webb (nee Jelly) of Mississauga, Ontario wasn't just competing to win the race. She was running for her father. Gerald Jelly died of pancreatic cancer just two weeks before the marathon, so Webb decided to run it in his honour. "He was hugely supportive of my running, and he would have been disappointed if I had not gone to the race," she says. But she remembers the conditions being anything but ideal. "It was very cold and windy at the start, and got worse during the race. After 30k, I just kept counting down the kilometres to the finish. I remember being so cold, but very happy to have finished and won the race." Webb finished in 2:52:03.

RETAIL FRENZY

A shortage of Tickle Me Elmo dolls caused Christmas chaos. In newspaper classifieds, the toys were advertised for hundreds of dollars. People magazine reported that the doll, with a retail price of $29, fetched as much as $1,500.

BYE BYE BILL

The Royal Canadian Mint unveiled the two-dollar coin. Initially, there was debate about what it would be called, but it quickly became known as the "toonie."

1997

706
marathon participants

🌡+14c

2:25:16
Nick Tsioros
Men's Winner

3:01:46
Laura Ruptash
Women's Winner

4,800
Race Weekend participants

Last-minute winner

Laura Ruptash wasn't planning to win the 1997 Ottawa Marathon. In fact, the day before the race, she wasn't even planning to enter the marathon. And even after she signed up at the last minute, she didn't intend to finish.

A friend of Ruptash's was coming from Montreal to run the marathon. "The day before he said, 'Why don't you run it with me?'" says Ruptash. "I told him, 'I'm not training for a marathon right now, so I'm not going to do it.' But finally I decided I would run the first half with him and get him through that."

Ruptash woke up on the morning of the marathon, cancelled Mother's Day brunch with her family, and headed to the start line, where she registered in the final minutes before the gun went off.

It's not like she was out of shape. Ruptash had won other races and was a competitive cyclist and triathlete. Her career had taken her to races in Europe, including a women's version of the Tour de France.

But she hadn't trained for the marathon, so winning – even finishing – was not on her mind. Indeed, she was so relaxed about the race that she even stopped to use a portable washroom in the first few kilometres.

"I thought, who cares, right?" she says. "I told him, 'I'll catch up with you later.'"

It's not the kind of the thing you do when you're trying to win a race. "Normally, if you're expecting to be competitive," says Ruptash, "you might dive behind a bush but not go to a port-a-potty."

When Ruptash and her friend made it to the halfway point, she was feeling good enough that she decided to continue.

"Why not keep going?" she remembers asking herself. "There's no pressure."

A lack of training is not the ideal prescription for winning a marathon. But maybe there's something to be said for arriving at an event with low expectations.

At the start line, Ruptash took note of another woman she figured was the favourite. "I thought, *there's your winner*," she says. "Partway through the second half I passed her. I remember thinking, 'Where does that put me?'"

Some time after that, she realized she was in the lead. "Pinch me," she says she thought to herself. "I can't believe this is happening to me today."

When Ruptash told her sister that she would be running the race instead of going to brunch with their mother, her sister said she and her husband might come out to watch.

"They weren't there the first time I passed. I thought, maybe they'll be there the second time. It would have been so great. I could have said, 'I'm in first.' But they didn't bother to get out of bed!"

Ruptash finished the race in just over three hours. She points out it's one of the slowest winning times in the history of the race. Indeed, the following year, when Ruptash actually trained for the marathon and finished five minutes faster than her winning time from 1997, the field was more competitive and she placed third.

However, even though she didn't break any records in winning the 1997 Ottawa Marathon, she still finished ahead of 164 other women to claim first place. Sometimes a little bit of luck and talent go a long way.

"I really wasn't expecting to do the marathon that day," she says. "I was expecting to help my friend."

"I can't believe this is happening to me today.

LAURA RUPTASH

BACK IN POWER

The Liberals, led by **Jean Chrétien**, were re-elected with a second majority in the 36th general election. Preston Manning became opposition leader.

THE STREAK ENDS

Four-time defending champion **Jean Lagarde** pulled out of the race at the 28-kilometre mark because of tight calf muscles, making way for **Nick Tsioros** of Aurora, Ontario, who was left to run solo for the rest of the race. It was the first marathon victory for the 28-year-old schoolteacher.

GREAT FEELING

After taking a four-month training program at the Running Room, blind runner Richard Marsolais of Ottawa finished his first marathon in four hours, 11 minutes, and 35 seconds. "It went quite well," says Marsolais, who was guided by six local runners, told the *Ottawa Citizen*. "Nothing hurt. It was such a great feeling to sprint to the finish over the last 200 metres."

PEOPLE'S PRINCESS

Diana, Princess of Wales, died on August 31, 1997, in a car crash in a Paris tunnel.

FOR ALL MUGGLES

British author J. K. Rowling released the first novel in the Harry Potter series, *Harry Potter and the Philosopher's Stone*.

"Not all marathon runners are able to finish the 42.2-kilometre distance, and those few completing the run are exhausted and barely moving their legs. This time we see that the winner, after a running time of three hours one minute, is laughing, with a gorgeous smile at the finishing line. What a marvellous sight! Being able to shuffle only a few metres with my old and stiff legs, I am in awe at the celebration of human potential in these marathons. If only the winner, Laura Ruptash, a massage therapist, could improve the performance of my legs to walk faster over Billings Bridge, to get to her Holistic Clinic at the Riverside Drive."

Nikolai G. Zoldners, in a letter to the *Ottawa Citizen*.

HIGH PRAISE

The Ultimate Guide to Marathons by Dennis Craythorn and Rich Hanna ranked the Ottawa Marathon 33rd out of all continental marathons based on course beauty and difficulty, appropriateness for first-timers, race organization, and crowds.

LONG WALK

Power walker David Lloyd-Pearce of Ottawa was the last competitor across the finish line, finishing his first marathon in 6:43.

FUTURE SAINT

Mother Teresa, the Nobel Peace Prize winner who devoted her life to helping the sick and the poor, died at the age of 87.

ROVING THE RED PLANET

NASA freed a robot from the Mars Pathfinder, allowing it to begin exploring the Red Planet.

WHERE ARE YOU?

Running a marathon was a bucket list item for Ottawa's **Gerry Thauvette**, one he wanted to complete before he was 40. In 1996, the then 39-year-old started training. When the race day came, he had a new girlfriend to cheer him on, but she wasn't on the sidelines when he completed the first loop of the course. "I was very disappointed that she was not there, and I bonked only a few kilometres into the second loop," he remembers. After finishing the race in 3:44, he found out his girlfriend, who later became his wife, had been in the massage tent. "When she realized she missed me, she went to the last 2k of the run and ran alongside me to make up for her oversight."

KING OF THE WORLD

The epic film *Titanic* was released. Directed, written, co-produced, co-edited, and partly financed by Canadian James Cameron, it was the most expensive film ever made at the time, with an estimated budget of more than $200 million.

1997

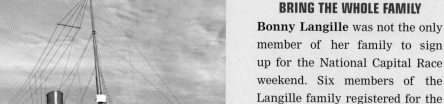

BRING THE WHOLE FAMILY

Bonny Langille was not the only member of her family to sign up for the National Capital Race weekend. Six members of the Langille family registered for the 2K and 6K Walk and Run, including Matthew Langille (bib number 6080). The two events were added to allow novice runners and walkers to share the running challenge with the marathoners.

1998

966

marathon participants

🌡 +19c

2:31:16

Malcolm Campbell

Men's Winner

2:49:06

Leslie Carson

Women's Winner

7,491

Race Weekemd participants

Follow the bunnies

When Hilda Beauregard ran the Chicago Marathon in 1997, she saw something she hadn't seen at other races: event organizers had provided pace bunnies to help amateur runners achieve their time goals.

An idea struck her right away. "I thought we should do the same thing in Ottawa," she says.

At the time, Beauregard was working for the Running Room. So when she returned home, she made the suggestion to the retail chain's founder, John Stanton, and Ottawa race director Jim Robinson. They were equally enthusiastic, and so, the next year, Beauregard launched a pace-bunny program.

She solicited volunteers who agreed to run the race in a specific time, letting other runners literally follow in their footsteps to the finish line. She even made the signs that the pace bunnies would carry so that other runners would know whom to follow. Her sister helped by getting them laminated.

Every year since, wearing caps with rabbit ears and carrying those clearly marked signs like the ones Beauregard made personally in 1998, the pace bunnies have been a regular component of the Ottawa Marathon. The program now covers all the major races at Ottawa Race Weekend and includes dozens of volunteers, many of whom have been pace bunnies for several years in a row.

Beauregard chose to be the 4:15 pace bunny in 1998. She had already run Ottawa many times by then, so serving as a guide for other runners helped to make it a fresh experience.

"It was amazing," she says. "I loved it. I had about 25 to 30 people starting out with me. By the end I had only five or six people. A few had gone ahead; some dropped off as we got to 28 to 30 kilometres."

There's more to the role of pace bunny than simply running. The group leaders also keep their runners upbeat, answer questions, and act as an unofficial tour guide for participants from out of town.

"You have to be the entertainment," says Beauregard. "You have to stay really positive and upbeat. And you have to totally focus on encouraging people not to quit."

Most of the volunteers who serve as pace bunnies can run much faster than their prescribed times, so they aren't too taxed when they are leading their groups. But it's still a marathon, and anything can happen.

Beauregard found herself in trouble the next year, when she signed up to be the 3:30 pace bunny.

"It was not my day," she says. "I brought them right on target to the halfway point, but then I said, 'I'm sorry I can't keep this up.' I had to take off my hat and let them go ahead."

Beauregard ended up finishing in 4:14, but she caught up with many of the runners from her group at the end of the race.

"They all came in around 3:30, 3:31, and 3:32," she says.

The role of pace bunny is one of the most visible in the race. The crowds along the route, especially younger spectators, give lots of encouragement to the runners wearing rabbit ears. And Beauregard has been inspired by the runners she's led. In one case, a runner who followed her to the finish line ended up training with her for the Boston Marathon the following year.

"I've met a lot of wonderful, amazing people that have run the marathon," she says. "I've heard a lot of great stories.

"I think it's amazing for anyone to run a marathon. It's very hard work."

Like the hundreds of pace bunnies who have followed her in leading other runners, Beauregard takes a lot of pleasure from the fact that she helped some of those amazing people get to the finish line on time.

SICK OF WINNING

Malcolm Campbell had no plans to run the 1998 Ottawa marathon until his former University of South Florida teammate, John Bowden of Toronto, called just three days before the race to invite him. The Scottish-born Campbell, traditionally a 5,000- and 10,000-metre runner, had run only two marathons before, but he won the race in 2:31:16, the slowest winning time in the marathon's history. After the race, Campbell was sick in the finish area, and vowed not to run another marathon again anytime soon.

GREAT NUMBER

Wayne Gretzky of the New York Rangers scored his 1,000th NHL goal (878 in the regular season and 122 in the playoffs) in a 6-3 Rangers loss to the Devils in New Jersey.

MAKING EVERYBODY FEEL LIKE HEROES

In a letter to the *Ottawa Citizen*, runner Fred Pelletier described the marathon and Ottawa Race Weekend as an outstanding success. "The city was treated to a well-planned, well-executed display of community spirit and teamwork," he wrote, adding that participants and spectators owed a debt of gratitude to race officials and "to the thousands of volunteers and supporters on the course who kept up their fine tradition of making everybody feel like heroes."

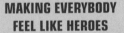

GO MOM!

It was a special Mother's Day for **Leslie Carson**, who won her first Ottawa Marathon. Although her three children didn't get to serve her breakfast in bed, they and her husband were on the sidelines watching and cheering as Carson won by almost five minutes. The dietician, who now lives in Whitehorse, retired from racing in 2005 after a hip injury, but she still follows the sport. "It's interesting following Krista DuChene, as she is a dietitian and mother of three like myself," she says. "When I hear how she's doing, it brings back memories of working full-time, being a mother and committed athlete. She has since taken over my long-standing title of 'fastest dietitian marathoner in Canada.'"

PERFORMANCE ENHANCER

Sildenafil citrate, better known by its commercial name Viagra, was approved for use in March 1998.

BIG FREEZE

Québec, Ontario and New Brunswick were hit with a major ice storm, leaving some residents without power for weeks.

AN UNLIKELY COINCIDENCE

When **Eric Martinat** showed his wife photos from the 1998 marathon in 2001, she was surprised to see two familiar faces in the shot with him. "Eric's friend snapped this picture with two other unknown runners in the frame," says Robyn Dicesare of Winnipeg. "After I met Eric, he showed me his photo album and I saw his picture. I said, 'Hey that's Roger and Angela!'" Angela Plamondon was Dicesare's best friend, and the two women had run together for the Ottawa Athletic Club. Her husband Roger was an RCMP officer and runner. "We're all still good friends today. I thought it amazing that the photo froze one split-second in time and it contained three of the people I hold dear."

Google

YOU COULD LOOK IT UP

Google Inc. was formall incorporated on September 4, 1998 in a garage in Menlo Park, California.

THE GANG'S ALL HERE

Toronto runner **Tom Irwin** didn't come alone to the marathon in 2011. Irwin brought along 35 runners from the Toronto Running Room with him. In the late 1990s, there was no spring marathon in the Toronto area, so for marathoners and half-marathoners looking for a race in the first half of the year, Ottawa was ideal. For a couple of years, Irwin's group would jump on a big yellow bus to make the trip and avoid the pain of driving post-marathon. "Back then, the marathon was held on Mother's Day weekend, which placed it in the heart of the tulip festival," says Irwin. He says he especially enjoyed running along the Rideau Canal.

1998

DOUBLE DUTY

Triathlete **Ian Fraser** of Ottawa didn't just pace the marathon. The night before the race, he also wore the bunny ears for the 10k race. Fraser served as the pace runner for 35:00 in the 10k and for three hours in the marathon.

MAY
9

1,378
marathon participants

+14c

2:22:24.7
Bruce Raymer
Men's Winner

2:39:56.4
Veronique Vandersmissen
Women's Winner

9,771
Race Weekend participants

Patience and perseverance

There are plenty of reasons not to run. And over the past 15 springs as she has prepared for the Ottawa Marathon, Louise Rachlis has encountered many of them.

One year, she had plantar fasciitis, a common but painful foot injury for runners. Another year, she was getting radiation treatment for a benign tumour. Then there was the time she was recovering from a fracture of the sternum suffered in a car accident. Another time her husband was getting hip replacement surgery.

"I've had a birth in the family, two deaths in the family, and a wedding in the family," she says. "And I always seem to have visitors at that time of year.

"Every single year, there's been something that has come up that could have been a reason not to run. And you can either say 'I'm not going to do the marathon,' and just quit. Or you can do it."

Rachlis has always chosen to do it. She's run the Ottawa Marathon every year since 1999.

Maybe that's because she overcame the biggest excuse of all: that she was too old to do a marathon. Rachlis didn't even start to run until after she'd turned 50.

She ran the 10k at Ottawa Race Weekend in 1998, and then helped out the next morning at the marathon. Her colleague at the *Ottawa Citizen*, Chris Macknie, was running his first marathon, and she was the volunteer who presented him with his medal at the end of the race.

"I thought that was pretty neat," she says. "I signed up for the half for the next year. Halfway through the training I thought, 'If I'm doing all this, I might as well do the marathon.'"

That first marathon went well. Rachlis describes it as "wonderful, exciting, and fun."

But she didn't have much time to celebrate. After crossing the finish line, she rushed back to the *Citizen* to put together the newspaper's special marathon section for the next day.

Once her work was complete and she had time to think about the race, she realized the significance of what she had done.

"I thought, 'Wow, if I can do a marathon I can do anything,'" she says. "And I proceeded to do anything. I started doing triathlons. I entered writing contests. I did feel empowered after doing it."

Rachlis says running has taught her patience and perseverance. She likes to call herself a back-of-the-pack runner. She says she'll probably never qualify for Boston, but she enjoys the camaraderie of runners who aren't racing to the finish line at top speed.

"You have to be more of a character to be at the back," she says. "You're doing the same distance. You're working just as hard. But it takes a different kind of courage than to be at the front."

Her enthusiasm and passion for running have inspired many others to take up the sport. Rachlis trains regularly with a group of runners she calls the Antiques of Steel. She says running keeps her feeling young. And she intends to keep running Ottawa every year for as long as she can.

"The good thing as you get older is that there are fewer people in your age group," she says. "I was third out of three last year, so maybe I can hang on until I'm 1 out of 1."

> **The good thing as you get older is that there are fewer people in your age group.**

LOUISE RACHLIS

FOR MOM

Paula Wiltse of Brockville, ON ran her first marathon with a special Mother's Day message on her back: "Happy Mother's Day Shirley Wiltse, Breast Cancer Survivor." At the time, her mother was getting treatment in Ottawa. "I saw the info on the race in the waiting room and started to train for it," she remembers. "Needless to say, I have been running ever since." Wiltse finished in seventh place in just over three hours and helped contribute to the $420,000 raised in 1999 for cancer treatment centres.

CURRENCY EVENTS

The Euro was launched on January 1, 1999, becoming the new official currency of 11 European countries and replacing old national currencies including the German Deutschmark and the French franc.

FRIENDLY MARATHON

For **Scott Hall** (bib number 836), it was his fourth time running Ottawa and also his slowest. But he had a good reason: he had run Boston just the month before. **Mike McLean** was one of the many friendly faces Hall encountered along the route. "That's probably one of the most attractive aspects of the Ottawa Marathon for me is that you get to race with your friends," says Hall.

PAINFUL RECOVERY

After signing up just days before the race, Ottawa's **Andrew Bridges** managed to complete his first marathon – but just barely. "I had signed up on an impulse the Friday before the race, and was completely unprepared, as my training consisted of cross country skiing and one four-hour run. I also had not heard of bandaids to protect my nipples, so my photo has significant red streaks on the front of the t-shirt. I had to go to a wake that evening, and remember not being able to walk down the stairs after my shower. I ended up sliding down on my butt. Having to stand for four hours in the receiving line was definitely not how I would recommend recovering from a marathon!"

SORRY ABOUT THAT, CHIEF

Mike Dyon might have been **Bruce Raymer**'s friend, training partner, and boss, but it didn't keep Raymer from beating the three-time champion. Raymer and Dyon, both of whom worked for Brooks Canada, were the leaders for the last 5k of the race. But in the end it was Raymer who crossed the finish line first. "It was hard," Raymer told the *Ottawa Citizen*. "For a minute there, I felt apologetic: 'I have to go now.'"

1999

RUNNING ROOM CONNECTION

Ottawa's **Hilda Beauregard** (bib number 390) met a familiar face at the 35-kilometre mark: **Catherine Adams**, the manager for the Beaches' Running Room in Toronto. "I was at that time the manager for the Slater Street Running Room in Ottawa," says Beauregard. "We ran into each other by sheer luck. We were so excited to see each other and were chatting so much that the last 7km just flew by. When we joined hands at the finish line it was such a fun and great feeling." See Beauregard's story in 1998.

TIME TO REPLENISH

She was fast, but second-place finisher **Tania Jones** spent almost as much time in the medical tent as she did on the course. After finishing her first marathon in 2:48:25.5, Jones needed five litres of fluids to help recover from hyperthermia and dehydration.

HELP!

A major blizzard hit the Midwest United States and parts of Eastern Canada early in the new year, dumping 118 centimetres of snow on Toronto and effectively closing the city. Mayor Mel Lastman called in the Canadian Forces for assistance, leading to jokes about Toronto for years to come.

NEW TERRITORY

Nunavut, Canada's northernmost territory, was born April 1, 1999.

DOUBLE WIN

Joyce Switzer (later Joyce Burghardt) not only became the first woman to win the Canadian military championships, but her fourth-place finish also secured the women's Masters title for runners 40 years old and over. The 42-year-old finished in 2:50:08. "I recall being quite awed at how in tune my body and mind felt to the extent that in the last 10k, usually the most difficult and painful portion of a marathon, I was thoroughly enjoying the cheers of the crowd, which included my coach Ken Parker and Ottawa Athletic Club Racing Club teammates, and the brilliant colours of the tulips along Queen Elizabeth Drive as we ran alongside the canal," says Burghardt.

Entrance to NAC Parking
Garage via Elgin and
Albert Streets

← Accès au stationnement
du CNA par les rues
Elgin et Albert

3:30

1978

0 00 00

NATIONAL CAPITAL
MARATHON

OFFICIAL PACE CAR

ONTARIO
SXX•519

1982

2002

1981

2004

Running for office

1,905
marathon participants

+15c

2:17:12.5
Bruce Deacon
Men's Winner

2:36:45.1
Veronique Vandersmissen
Women's Winner

11,500
Race Weekend participants

It's not unusual for elected officials to hear both jeers and cheers when they appear in public. So when John Manley ran his first marathon in Ottawa in 2000, he wasn't sure what kind of reception he would receive.

"You worry a little bit as a politician about the reaction you're going to get," says Manley, who was then the federal minister of industry. "You see people going out to drop the puck at a hockey game and they get booed. But the response in the running community was unanimously positive. Not a single negative. People were thanking me for running. It was a great reinforcement of what I was doing."

After the race, Manley even heard from constituents telling him he had inspired them to try the marathon.

"They said, 'When I realized that as a minister you have time to do it, I figured, what excuse do I have?'" says Manley.

Manley says he started training for a marathon because it was on his bucket list. But he came to appreciate the solitude, which was rare in his busy life as a cabinet minister.

"What I discovered was that, as a minister, one of the great challenges is the lack of private time, time alone to think things through and to reflect on things," he says. "The training became my outlet for time to think and get my bearings."

A few times a week, taking advantage of the fact that he had a car and driver, he would have his briefcase and clothes picked up at his house in the morning and he would run to the office.

"It usually took about 50 minutes," he said. "You start doing that a few days a week, plus a long run on the weekend, and you're already well on your way to training for a marathon."

And he made it very clear to his staff that his training runs were non-negotiable.

"I had to discipline my staff that I needed at least an hour and a quarter in my schedule every day. They had to realize that even if there wasn't room in there, I was going to do it anyway.

"I remember one time I was 45 minutes late for something because I went for my run. I had a marathon I had to get ready for. I was very sorry but I had to discipline everyone around me that this was very important to me and I was going to do it."

On more than one occasion during his career in cabinet, Manley would arrive at work sweating in his running clothes, and the security staff at the front desk wouldn't recognize him.

"They don't give you a pass like everyone else," he says. "The security people are expected to recognize the minister. Well, here's a guy showing up in a sweat band and running clothes. They say, 'Let me see your pass.' And I'd say, 'I don't have one, but there's my picture on the wall.' That's not the way they're expecting the minister to arrive."

Manley has run a total of five marathons. Along with his debut in Ottawa, the one that stands out the most for him is when he ran New York City less than two months after September 11, 2001. He organized a gathering of Canadian runners before the race and gave them all t-shirts with a maple leaf, a heart and "NY" on them.

But crossing the finish line of his first marathon in his hometown is a memory he continues to cherish.

"It was amazing," he says, "The whole experience was a real thrill. It's a rush of excitement and satisfaction that you prepared for it and you executed and you did it.

"And what a magnificent event this has grown into for the city. People all over the world ask me about it. This has got to be one of the best places to run in the world."

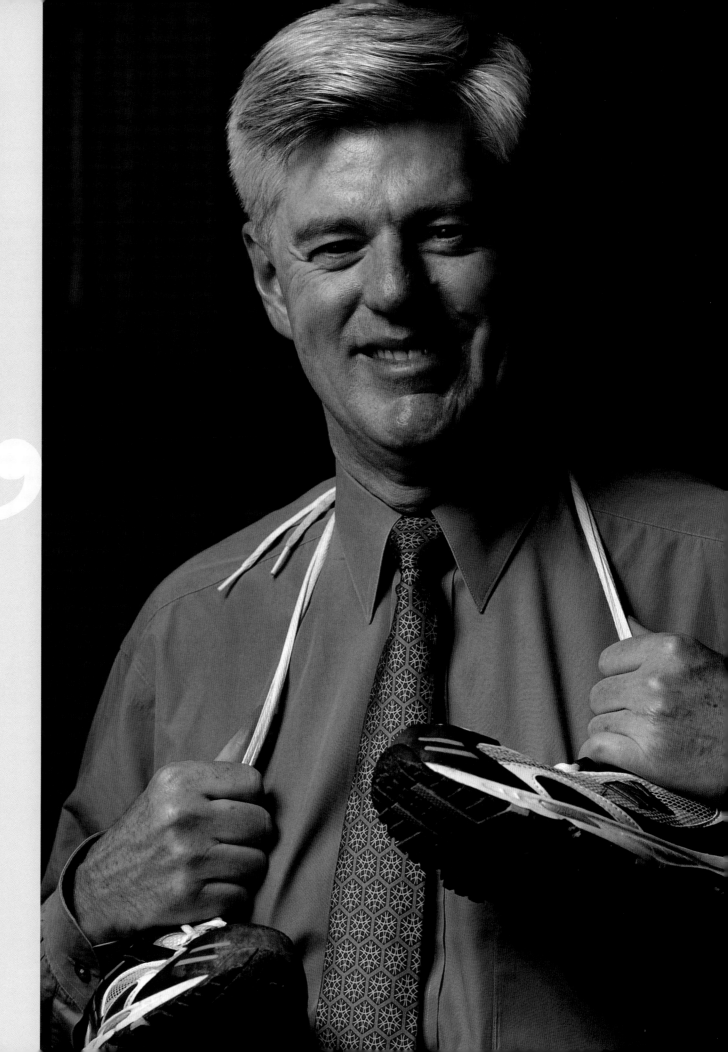

"This has got
to be one
of the best
places to run
in the world."

JOHN MANLEY

GOLDEN MOMENT

At the first Olympic triathlon in Sydney, the winner was Canadian **Simon Whitfield**.

FAMILY BUSINESS

Hillary Rodham Clinton, wife of former president Bill Clinton, became the first former First Lady to win a seat in the U.S. Senate.

END OF A CHAPTER

Pierre Elliot Trudeau died on September 28, 2000 at the age of 80.

A TRIUMPHANT RETURN

Twenty-one years after running Ottawa as a 12-year-old, **Bruce Deacon** won the marathon in 2:17:12.5. That's an hour and 13 minutes faster than his time in 1979.

2000

WINNERS DOWN UNDER

Gezahegne Abera of Ethiopia won gold in 2:10:11 in the men's Olympic marathon in Sydney. Canada's Bruce Deacon came in 44th in 2:21:38. Japan's Naoko Takahashi's time of 2:23:14 set an Olympic record in the women's race.

ENCORE

Veronique Vandersmissen of Coteau du Lac, Quebec did not make the Olympic women's standard of 2:33, but she did defend her title with a time of 2:36:45. Tania Jones finished second for the second year in a row, but this year stayed out of the medical tent. See Tania's story in 2002.

ALONE AT THE TOP OF HER CLASS

Valerie Kilpatrick's first marathon went even better than planned. She'd hoped to complete the race in a time between four-and-a-half and five hours. But the woman from Monkland, Ontario crossed the finish line in 4:20:20.3, winning her age group. Of course, she was the only woman in the 60-64 category. But her run was still impressive and inspired her to come back in 2001, 2004, and 2005.

2001

Appealing to the gods

Unlike other 12-year-olds in the late 1970s, Bruce Deacon didn't dream of winning the Stanley Cup. His goal was to run in the Olympic Marathon. And his hero wasn't a hockey superstar, but legendary runner Bill Rodgers.

"He was my Bobby Orr," says Deacon. "When other kids were pretending they were Bobby, I was thinking to myself, 'I want to be like Bill Rodgers.'"

So after completing a couple of marathons as a boy, he wrote to Rodgers, who won Boston and New York four times each. Rodgers replied, but it wasn't the response Deacon was looking for.

"He said, 'You should be doing shorter races,'" says Deacon. "That was not the message I wanted to hear. The thing I had was that I could run longer races, not faster. But I took his advice and stopped running marathons at 12, and started running track and cross-country races."

Deacon's early interest in running began after the 1976 Olympics in Montreal.

"After the Olympics, everyone was enthusiastic about sport," he says. "But I was one of the smallest kids in my class. I wasn't very co-ordinated. I was the guy who went in the out-field because nobody could hit the ball that far."

So Deacon made a deal with God.

"I started praying," he said. "Find me a sport I can do well at, and I promise I'm going to work really hard at it."

At summer camp, he stumbled upon running. One of the counsellors was a marathoner who set up a running club. Every camper who ran 30 miles over the course of the summer would be given a t-shirt.

"I had no clue what a marathon was," says Deacon. "I figured if I could get him alone on a run I could find out what it was."

So Deacon asked to join the counsellor on one of his regular five-mile runs. There was only one problem: Deacon had never run that far.

"I wouldn't say it was a lie," he says. "But up until then, the farthest I'd run was across schoolyard, playing tag."

Deacon decided to try running 10 laps of a half-mile loop around the camp to see if he could go five miles without stopping.

"I thought 'if I stop, it doesn't count,'" he says. "And I did it. I didn't stop. I thought, 'I bet you there's a lot of other kids that can't do that. Maybe this is the sport for me.'"

Deacon started running almost every morning, doing as many laps as he could on a 400-metre loop on school grounds. "Next thing you know, I'd be arriving before school and running 10 miles," he says.

A family friend helped him design a marathon program, and in 1979, he ran Ottawa, finishing in three-and-a-half hours. He told his mother after the race that he would one day run the marathon in the Olympics, which he did in 1996 and 2000.

But first, on the advice of his hero, Deacon took an 11-year break from marathons, not running another until he was 23. Eventually, he found his way back to Ottawa, where he won the marathon in 2000. His mother Gail described it to the *Ottawa Citizen* as "quite a Mother's Day gift."

It was also somewhat of a historic win. As of 2014, Deacon is the last Canadian to win Ottawa. In 2001, the race began attracting international athletes through its elite program that offered significant prize money. Deacon finished second to the race's first African winner, Joseph Nderitu, in both 2001 and 2002. He was also the last Canadian in the Olympic marathon until the London Games in 2012.

Whether he won or not, getting a chance to run in his hometown was always important to Deacon.

"A lot of my races were happening elsewhere in the world," he says. "My family didn't really have a chance to see those races. For my grandmother and my parents to see me run at home was really quite significant."

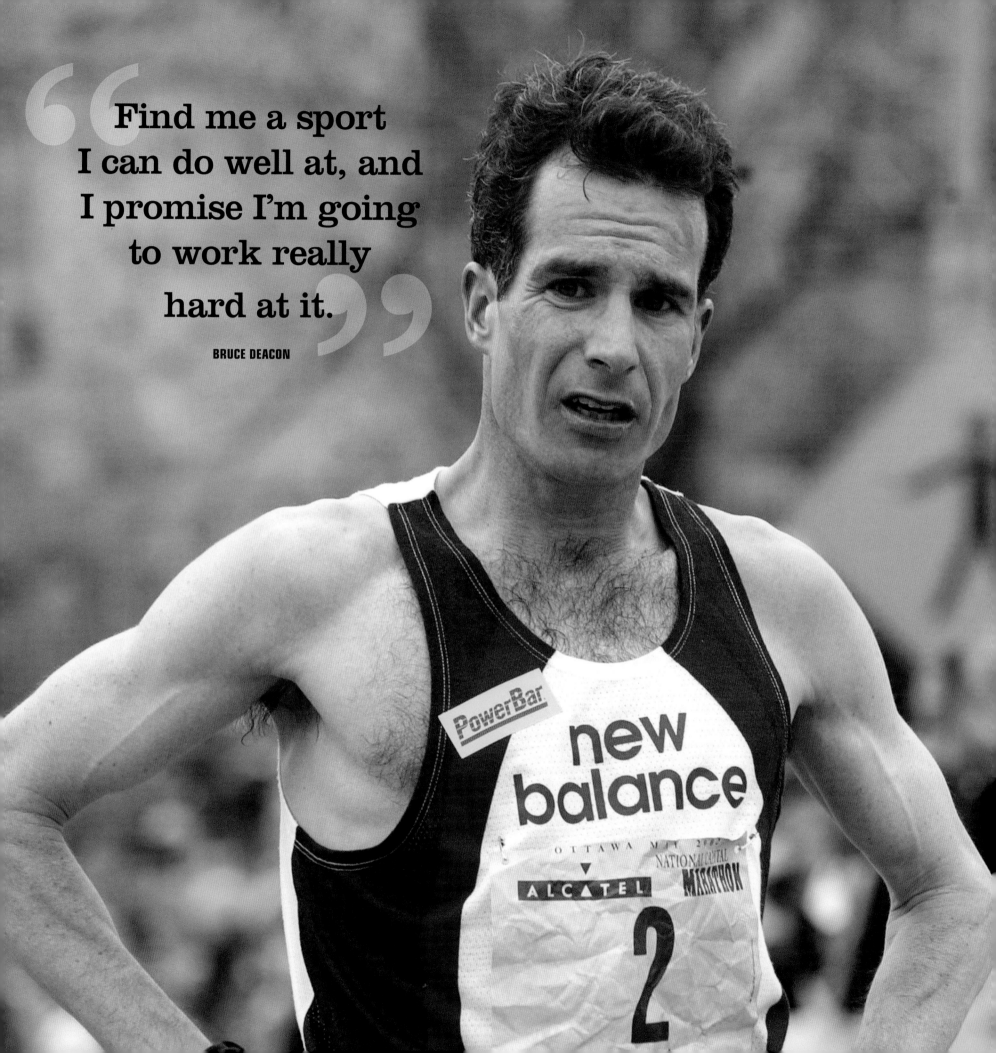

> "Find me a sport I can do well at, and I promise I'm going to work really hard at it."
>
> BRUCE DEACON

ELITE COMPANY

Joseph Nderitu of Kenya became the first African to win the Ottawa Marathon as the elite era began. Nderitu's time of 2:15:50 was the fourth-best winning time in the marathon's 27-year history. It was Nderitu's eighth North American race in seven weeks. He was awarded $5,000 for winning the race and $5,000 for eclipsing the bonus standard of 2:16.

LITERARY TIGER

Life of Pi, by Yann Martel, was published in 2001 after being rejected by at least five London publishing houses. It was awarded the Booker Prize the following year.

FALLING TO ONE KNEE AT THE FINISH

Jeramie Carbonaro wasn't just worried about finishing the 2001 marathon. He was nervous about what would happen after it. After crossing the finish line 33rd overall, the 26-year-old got down on one knee and asked his girlfriend Forest Heggie to marry him. "It was the perfect time to propose," Carbonaro told the *Ottawa Citizen*. "It was the end of one race and the beginning of another. I thought she would be really surprised." The marriage proposal was the first in the event's 27-year history. And it paid off. The Windsor, Ontario couple is still happily married, with two children.

PEDAL TO THE MEDAL

Organizers added a kids' scooter race and 10-year-old **Mark Dicesare** was one of those who pedaled his way to the finish.

REMEMBERING 9/11

Just weeks after the terroist attacks of September 11, more than 23,000 runners finished an emotional New York City Marathon.

PROUD TO PASS THE TEST

Joyce Burghardt (formerly Joyce Switzer) placed fifth overall and won the Canadian Women's Military Championship for the second time. "The one aspect of this marathon that I always remember so vividly as being special is that I had made the cut to be drug tested. I was absolutely thrilled with this," she says. It did mean missing all the festivities right after the race because, as Burghardt says, it takes a bit of time to "produce a sample" when you are dehydrated at the end of a marathon.

2001

SHOELESS SORO

Barefoot runner **Bassirima Soro** of Kenya finished fifth in 2:24:15.

GOING TO POT

Canada became the first country in the world to legalize medical marijuana.

ATTENTION MALL COPS

The Segway Personal Transporter, the world's first electric, two-wheeled, self-balancing transportation device, was unveiled.

KNOW WHEN TO WALK AWAY, KNOW WHEN TO RUN

Danuta Bartoszek of Mississauga, Ontario caught **Sandy Jacobson** in the final two kilometres and pulled ahead to win in 2:37:58.9. Although she won in 2001, Bartoszek says the race in 2002, when she placed third, was even more memorable. "This was to be my last race ever," she says. "I had decided to retire after Ottawa. Not an easy decision, but my running career had been a long and successful one, with many happy memories. Over the closing miles of that final race maybe I started to reflect on that and as Tania [Jones] closed in on me in and I went from second to third overall, I accepted that I had made the right decision and it was okay to be beaten by someone younger."

Graduation day

After winning the Canadian title in Ottawa in 2002, Tania Jones felt like she had finally arrived as a marathon runner.

"I can call myself a true marathoner," she told reporters after the race. "I belong now. I've mastered it, in a way. I've got the hang of it."

Picking up on her comments in the *Ottawa Citizen* the next day, Martin Cleary wrote, "There was no special gown or ceremony or diploma, but Tania Jones graduated yesterday as a certified marathon runner."

It wasn't just that Jones achieved her goal of being the top Canadian and also finished second overall. For the first time at the marathon distance, she was happy with how she performed throughout the race.

In 1999, Jones made her marathon debut in Ottawa. She finished second in that race; she'd been leading the race for part of the second half, but she struggled a great deal in the final few kilometres.

"That first marathon, I messed it up," she says. "I came second overall, but I ended up in the medical tent. I walked part of it. It just beat me to death. I was in really bad shape."

Jones was in the medical tent for more than two hours, and was administered five litres of fluid to treat her dehydration.

"I have more to learn about it," she told the *Citizen* after the race. "It's a new game. I thought I could nail it the first time."

Jones finished second again in 2000, and this time required no medical attention. But she was still disappointed with her performance, particularly because, once again, she ran out of energy near the end of the race.

In 2002, that didn't happen. Drawing on her past experiences, she didn't go out as quickly in the first half of the race, and saved something for the last few kilometres. That came in handy as she fought off a late charge from the second-place Canadian woman, who finished just 10 seconds behind her.

"By 2002, I had a lot more experience, and I had made a lot of mistakes," said Jones. "I was able to dig deep. She almost caught me."

Jones lived in Ottawa from 1994 to 1998, a time she says was the foundation of her running career. She trained with the Ottawa Lions Club, and met many of the other runners who were blossoming at that time.

"Ottawa really launched my career," she says. "The running culture there, the running community were a huge factor. Also, having that really good-quality racing event to focus on every spring."

Jones won the Ottawa 10k in 1995 and then defended her title in 1996, setting a course record. She finished third in 1997, and lost by a tenth of a second in 1998.

Even after she moved to the Toronto area, Jones still felt strong ties to Ottawa, and competed often at Race Weekend events.

"I always felt that there was that hometown feel to the event," she says. "There was always a connection for me. It was a race where people would yell my name on the street. That's a nice feeling.

"And I always admired that the race changed and grew; they've brought in the international competition, and have tried to have the deepest field of Canadian runners. It's nice not to have to travel to some faraway city to have that."

Looking back more than 10 years later, Jones still regards the 2002 Ottawa Marathon as a breakthrough race, one of the best of her career.

"I finally conquered the marathon with that one," she says. "To come home and win the Canadian championship was the culmination of a lot of things. We finally got it all together. And it was a big sense of relief to have closed a marathon properly."

"It was a race where people would yell my name on the street. That's a nice feeling.

TANIA JONES

SPRINT TO THE FINISH

Eric Martinat may not have been the first runner to cross the finish line, but you wouldn't have known it by his stride. According to his wife Robyn, as the clock was ticking up to 3:03, Martinat sprinted hard to the finish. "The announcer was going crazy, and the crowd was cheering like he was about to win the race. For him, it was of those magic moments that comes along only a few times in your life."

NUMBER TEN, AGAIN!

Dave Turgeon of St-Foy, Quebec placed 10th for the third year in a row, shaving minutes off his time and achieving another personal best. But 10th was a big jump from Turgeon's first appearance at the marathon in 1999, when he finished 107th.

"Two weekends ago, I travelled to Ottawa from Halifax to run my first full marathon. While I came alone, with no family or friends to cheer me along the route, I was made to feel like a true champion by the fans and spectators. To the many people who gave up their Sunday morning to support us: Thank you. I applaud you."

Darren Currie of Halifax, in a letter to the *Ottawa Citizen*.

GOLDEN MEN AND WOMEN

Canada won men's and women's hockey gold at the 2002 Winter Olympics in Salt Lake City. And after initially being awarded silver, **Jamie Salé and David Pelletier** were given pairs figure skating gold after a judging scandal.

OPENING THE BODY

After completing her first marathon in 2001 with almost no proper training, Ottawa's **Andrea Robertson** decided to try again in 2002. Of her first attempt, which she finished in a time of 4:09, Robertson says, "It was a really warm day, and I remember feeling very proud that I actually did it! I also remember not being able to walk for days." Despite better preparation, Robertson finished her second marathon in 4:41 because of a knee injury. But that marathon helped propel her down a new path. "I committed myself to yoga and opening my body. I completed my yoga teacher training in 2004, and have been teaching for 10 years." Robertson produced her own DVD of yoga for runners.

OUTBREAK

The first cases of severe acute respiratory syndrome (SARS) were found in Southern China. A total of 8,098 people worldwide became sick with SARS during the outbreak the following year, 774 died.

LOOKING STRONG

Emma Stodel knows a thing or two about how to prepare psychologically for running a marathon. Stodel, a mental training consultant, works with runners, golfers, and skiers on their preparation. During the 2002 marathon, Stodel applied some of her knowledge to herself. "My running partners and I had a plan: rounding Dow's Lake, with 6k to go, we would decide whether to pick up the pace and kick for home, or just try to hang on and make it to the finish line. I looked over at the others as we started down Queen Elizabeth Drive. After 36k, they still looked strong and fresh. I thought I'd be running the home stretch alone. With gritted determination, I pushed on to achieve a Boston qualifying time. At the finish line, my running buddies commented on how strong I looked and how worried they were about holding me back. How we feel on the inside doesn't always show on the outside!"

FAST AT 46, AND 50

At the age of 46, Toronto's **Lynn Kobayashi** finished in 3:07:02, 30 minutes faster than her first Ottawa marathon in 1982. "It was an all-time PB, and my best masters time by five minutes. It was exhilarating, and kept me motivated to train hard and be in great shape for the marathon when I turned 50. I ran 3:10:09 in Detroit four days after I turned 50. That time was an Ontario 50-54 record for the marathon that stood for six years."

Run for the son

MAY
11

3,068
marathon participants

+14c

2:15:29.2
Joseph Nderitu
Men's Winner

2:33:51.9
Sandy Jacobson
Women's Winner

20,328
Race Weekend participants

Facing a long and humbling recovery from brain surgery, Angelo Talluto decided he had to do something bold to snap himself out of his doldrums. And even though he had never run a race before, completing the Ottawa Marathon became the goal he seized upon to turn his life around.

Talluto was 30 years old and his wife was seven months pregnant when, early one morning in June 2002, he fell out of bed and went into seizure.

"My wife tells me I said, 'I can't breathe, I can't breathe,'" says Talluto. He was rushed to hospital, where doctors discovered a massive brain tumour. The tumour wasn't cancerous, but the surgeon said it was one of the biggest he'd seen. He operated on Talluto one week later.

The recovery was even more difficult than expected. Talluto was in hospital for weeks, he suffered from seizures, and found the medication to be debilitating. Talluto says he became depressed when he realized how long it was going to take to get back to normal.

But when his son A.J. was born, everything changed.

"I didn't see the reason to live after having the brain tumour," he says. "I wanted to get myself back in shape. I wanted to go to work. But I was helpless.

"And once he was born, that became my reason to live. He saved my life."

Talluto says that before his surgery, he played hockey and stayed in good shape, but he had never run more than three kilometres at once. Nevertheless, when he stumbled upon the Ottawa Marathon while searching the Internet one day, he knew that's what he had to do.

"I thought, 'That's it, that's what I'm doing,'" he says.

But he told no one. He started going for walks, and then began adding in incremental amounts of running. At first he felt dizzy, but eventually he could run five or six kilometres without stopping. A few months before the marathon, he decided to embark on a full training plan.

"I finally told my wife," he says. "She thought I was crazy. My family thought it was the medication that was making me crazy to want to do this. But I knew I had to. This was the only way."

And when he told one of the doctors who had helped him, a neuroscientist named Dave Holden, he got a surprising response. Rather than try to talk him out of it, Holden said he would join him on the run.

Halfway through the race, Talluto says he thought about everything he'd been through in the past year. With about 10k to go, Holden told him to go on without him.

"He said, 'I'm struggling, you go for it,'" says Talluto. "He gave me some inspirational words and told me how much he admired me and told me to go for it. So I did."

The last two kilometres were tough, and Talluto was weak enough at the finish line that he was taken to the medical tent. But he accomplished his goal, only 11 months after his surgery.

In the decade since the marathon, Talluto has made a full recovery. He's run a handful of other marathons and is now a phys-ed teacher. He and his wife have since had another son.

But at the time of the race, Talluto didn't know what the future held. His life was still in upheaval. He wasn't allowed to drive, and was still on medication that made him agitated. He worried that he wouldn't be around to see his son grow up.

So he felt compelled to run as a legacy for A.J.

"I did it for my son," he says. "If something happened to me, he would look back on this and remember what his Dad did.

"Doing the marathon was a message to him and to me that things are going to happen, bad things. And what's the choice you're going to make? Are you going to let it defeat you, or are you going to take it on?

"I decided, 'What's the craziest way I can take this on? Doing the marathon.'"

"I did it for my son.

ANGELO TALLUTO

BEST OF THE YEAR

Dan Brown's *The Da Vinci Code* was the best-selling fiction book of 2003.

THREE-PEAT CHAMPION

Joseph Nderitu joined Mike Dyon and Gord Christie as a three-time winner of the Ottawa Marathon. Only Jean Legarde has won more, with four straight victories. Fellow Kenyan Joseph Kamau played a big part in Nderitu's victory as the hired pace rabbit who helped pace Nderitu to a finish of 2:15:29.2.

"As a marathon participant, I cannot find words adequate enough to express my appreciation for the volunteers at the water and first aid stations, and the people who lined the route cheering the runners on. You made the difference. Race Weekend is a marvelous event, one [of] which all of Ottawa deserves to be very proud."

Brian R. O'Neal, in a letter to the *Ottawa Citizen*.

BOX OFFICE RUN

Finding Nemo was released on May 30, 2003. It went on to be the second-highest-grossing movie of the year, and won the Academy Award for best animated feature.

BIG IMPROVEMENT

Sandy Jacobson of Edmonton was the women's winner, chopping more than four-and-a-half minutes from her personal best time and finishing in 2:33:51.9.

SHEPHERDS ON BIKES

Angela Stiles, a 28-year-old runner from Dartmouth, Nova Scotia, finished her first marathon in last place, in six hours, 42 minutes, and 50 seconds. What Stiles remembers most about the day is a volunteer named Heidi. "She was part of the medical support team. She was on a bicycle and, [it] being evident that I was the back of the pack, she rode alongside me while I kept moving forward. She was so supportive. I felt badly that I was holding her up and for taking so long, but she just kept saying that it was okay. As we kept passing by different medical station points, we kept picking up a new cyclist from that area. By the end of the race, I had a small troop of medical team cyclists by my side. They were my cheering squad at the finish, and I will always remember their support that day. But Heidi was with me the longest, and I was so grateful to be able to give her a hug at the finish line."

2003

SIMPLY THE BEST

British runner **Paula Radcliffe** set the women's world record for the marathon at the 2003 London Marathon with a time of 2:15:25. Radcliffe won London three times, the New York City Marathon twice, and the Chicago Marathon once.

RUNNER AND LEADER

Michelle Standen Elston ran her second marathon, shaving 45 minutes off her time from the Vancouver Marathon the year before. "I participated in Ottawa Race Weekend a number of times, and each one has a story that holds a special place in my heart. I am also very proud of the fact that I had the opportunity to lead Running Room running clinics in order to prepare many runners to cross the finish line at this event as well."

YOU'VE COME A LONG WAY

Marathon legends **Kathrine Switzer** and Frank Shorter were both at the Ottawa Marathon in 2003, speaking at the fitness expo. In 1967, Switzer became the first woman to enter and run the Boston Marathon. Her entry got worldwide attention when a race official tried to remove her forcibly from the race. Shorter is the American runner who won the gold medal in the marathon at the 1972 Summer Olympics. Shorter moderated a panel featuring Switzer, runner Tania Jones, and Canadian Olympican Silvia Ruegger on the evolution of women's running.

BROTHER ACT

The Ottawa Marathon has been part of the lives of **Jacques** and **Pierre Caplette** of Anjou, Quebec for more than a quarter of a century. Jacques made his first appearance at the marathon in 1977, and his brother joined him in 1978. In 2003 in Ottawa, Pierre completed his 200th marathon and Jacques ran his 100th and last marathon.

READY THUMBS

Blackberry released its first smartphone.

The marathon moms

MAY
30

4,330
marathon participants

+18c

2:11:47.4
Elly Rono
Men's Winner

2:30:53.0
Lioudmila Kortchaguina
Women's Winner

23,150
Race Weekend participants

When Hazel Green's son Michael was diagnosed with leukemia in 1999, just before his fifth birthday, one of the greatest challenges she faced was that he often refused to take his chemotherapy treatment.

"We had to hold him down a lot," she says. "We had to pry his fingers off the car door, then pry them off the door to the hospital. If you let him go, he'd run away."

As Hazel struggled with her son, another mother offered to help. Elaine Vizena's son Jamie, who was diagnosed with an aggressive form of leukemia when he was eight, was getting treatment on the same cycle as Michael.

"She was very supportive of me," says Green. "She had been going through it just a little bit longer, and she became such a good support system."

Over the next few years, the mothers became friends. And they eventually spent time together at Camp Trillium, a recreational facility for children with cancer. It was there that the idea of running a marathon was hatched.

Vizena was a runner, but she had never done a long-distance event. She decided she wanted to do something significant in response to all the support she'd received while Jamie was being treated.

"I had made some promises to myself and to God that I was going to give back to everybody that helped me and my son when he was getting treatment," she says.

After watching her son and Hazel's go through chemotherapy, a marathon to raise money for Camp Trillium seemed like the least they could do.

"If our kids can suffer through this, we can do it," says Vizena. "This is nothing compared to what they went through."

The camp was a natural fit for their fundraising. Both Michael and Jamie survived cancer and are adults now. But when they were going through treatment and recovery, the camp was a place where the families found relief from stress and a chance to have fun.

"Before we went there, we were scared to let Michael do anything," says Green. "At the camp, we learned that he could fall down and he would be okay. It gave us a sense of normalcy. So it was the perfect thing to fundraise for."

There was one detail that needed to be addressed: Green wasn't a runner.

"I was a major couch potato," she says.

"Hazel had never done five minutes of exercise in her life," says Vizena. "She looked at me like I had four heads. But by the end of the week I had convinced her."

Over the next few months, the women began training. But Green lived in Petawawa, Vizena in Ottawa. So they weren't able to run together often.

"We would call each other two or three times a week and see how our running was going," says Vizena. "Every two months we'd get together for a run; I'd drive up there or she'd come here, so we knew we were on the same pace."

"The training was really hard," says Green. She remembers having a hard time getting out of the car the evening after a long run.

"But she was phenomenal," says Vizena. "For someone who had never exercised, to stick with it and be motivated? I was so proud of her."

"She really pushed me along," says Green.

Unfortunately, Vizena was injured a few weeks before the race and ended up walking a large portion of the course.

"She was in so much pain, I didn't know how she would do it," says Green.

But the marathon moms, as they called themselves, finished the race, and together they raised almost $10,000 for the camp. Green's parents pledged $20 if she started, and $1,000 if she made it to the finish line.

"I actually couldn't believe I did it," says Green.

"She amazed me," says Vizena. "My run was horrific. It was awful. But I was really happy for Hazel. I was glad we had raised all this money. I'm glad we followed through."

> I was glad we had raised all this money. I'm glad we followed through.

ELAINE VIZENA

A NEW SPONSOR

ING became the title sponsor of the Ottawa Marathon. The race was also designated as the host of the 2004 Canadian National Marathon Championship by Athletics Canada, making it a qualifier for the 2004 Summer Olympics in Athens.

30 IS THE NEW MARATHON

For the marathon's 30th edition, the race received a bit of a make-over. Organizers changed the date from the traditional Mother's Day weekend to the last weekend of May. The two-loop course was replaced by a scenic interprovincial route that took runners past or near nine of Ottawa's top tourist sites, and over three Ottawa-Gatineau bridges. And the time was adjusted to 7:00 a.m. – one hour earlier – to take advantage of cooler morning temperatures and allow Ottawa's streets to reopen sooner.

GRETE THE GREAT

Ottawa runners welcomed marathon legend **Grete Waitz**. The great Norwegian spoke at the fitness expo, attended the pasta dinner and the start of the 10k race Saturday, and helped launch the marathon runners Sunday. Waitz set four marathon world records in her career, was the nine-time New York City Marathon women's champion, and was the first woman to break two hours and 30 minutes.

HAPPY MARATHON TO YOU

Richard Borsos of Ottawa gave credit to the crowds after running a 3:02 marathon at 52 years of age. It was his sixth Ottawa Marathon. At one point when he was running near the National Gallery of Canada, he says a group of young women were singing Happy Marathon to the tune of Happy Birthday. On another corner, there was a group of belly dancers moving to their own music.

AU REVOIR BASEBALL

The Expos played their last game in Montreal on September 29, 2004.

I RUN, I COACH

Mark Sullivan ran the Ottawa Marathon for the first time in 2004. The prolific runner and coach has run it every year since, among more than 160 marathons in his career. Sullivan describes Ottawa as one of his favourites because "the marathon course is beautiful and, more importantly, fast." He also points to the fact that, unlike other large events, the start line is within walking distance of downtown hotels. "It's a marathon that is very conducive to a good race time," he says. "Being able to walk right to the start provides a perfect warm-up, and helps you stay calm by avoiding traffic or parking issues. In addition, the course is relatively flat, with plenty of volunteers and aid stations."

2004

facebook.

SMART GUY
Ken Jennings won 74 games in a row on the game show *Jeopardy!*, collecting $2.5 million.

THE FACEBOOK
Facebook was founded on February 4, 2004 by Mark Zuckerberg and his Harvard roommates.

LOVE AT THE FINISH LINE
Bryan Krasovskis of Niagara Falls, Ontario worked with race officials so he could propose to his girlfriend at the finish line. "I had to tell my wife (then girlfriend) that I put myself into a draw where you could have a loved one sit in the VIP booth and wait for the other to cross the finish line," remembers Krasovskis. "It was a great experience, and I enjoyed the Ottawa Marathon, and one day I would like to run it again."

LOTS OF RUNNING
In 2004, **Walter Robinson** scratched two things off his "to do" list. "I ran in the federal election and in my first Ottawa Marathon," he says. "I really only trained on Sundays, given all the walking and door-knocking I was doing, and ran 4:28." Robinson says he was in pain for a week after the race. "This experience returned me to running, and I've competed in dozens of halfs and 10k races since. I hope the Ottawa Race Weekend goes for another 40 years; it is a community-building and -defining event."

THINKING FOR YOU
Adidas released the Adidas 1 – a thinking running shoe with a built in microprocessor that decides how soft or firm a degree of support the wearer needs.

Grateful to run

MAY
29

4,197
marathon participants

+16c

2:14:20.3
David Cheruiyot
Men's Winner

2:31:52.7
Lidiya Vasilevskaya
Women's Winner

24,100
Race Weekend participants

What gives someone the inspiration to try a marathon? For Cheryl Kardish-Levitan, the original impetus came from a chance encounter with another runner in Jamaica in 1975. But more recently, it became something much more personal: a way of proving she had fully recovered from breast cancer.

Forty years ago, Kardish-Levitan was running a few times a week on the track at Carleton University.

"I was doing three-and-a-half miles," she says. "I thought that was huge."

On a trip to the Caribbean in December 1975, she went for a run and made a new friend.

"I see this slim guy running toward me. He said, 'Do you mind if I run with you?' I said, 'Sure, no problem.'

"He said, 'I'm just coming back from an 18-mile run. I'm a marathon runner.' And I said, 'What's a marathon runner?'"

The man, who was an American secret service agent working at an international summit in Jamaica, offered to help Kardish-Levitan build her mileage. So over the course of the next two weeks in Jamaica, the pair ran together, and Kardish-Levitan ramped up to 10 miles per run.

"He was my mentor. And when I came back to Ottawa, I started training for the marathon."

Kardish-Levitan ran the Ottawa Marathon for the first time in 1976, the second year of the event. She crossed the finish line third among women.

"It's not that I was fast. It's just there was no competition," she says.

She became a passionate runner, completing a total of 20 marathons and dozens of other races over the next decade. She became a fixture along the regular running routes in Ottawa, including the path beside the Rideau Canal. And she often heard from other women whom she inspired to take up running just because they saw her out on the roads.

"I've had a lot of women come up to me and say I had a positive impact on them," she says.

After 1976, Kardish-Levitan ran Ottawa every year up to and including 1984, when she finished it while three months pregnant with her first child.

Over the course of the next 15 years, while raising three children, she scaled back to half-marathons and shorter races. She wasn't sure she would ever run another marathon. But in 2000, Kardish-Levitan was diagnosed with breast cancer.

"That's when I said I would really like to do another marathon," she says. "It was my way of dealing with cancer. If I could just stay in shape to do another marathon, then I knew I was okay."

In 2005, 20 years after her last marathon, Kardish-Levitan finally ran Ottawa again.

"It was very emotional for me to do that," she says. "To be able to come back and do it, I was ecstatic. I was crying at the finish line."

Having participated in the early years and more recently, Kardish-Levitan has seen the Ottawa Marathon evolve over almost 40 years.

"I can understand why it attracts more and more people," she says. "It's a beautiful course, it's the nation's capital, it takes in the most attractive sites that Ottawa can offer. And it's the warmth of the people, the volunteers, the camaraderie."

Kardish-Levitan has run many different events, but when she enters Ottawa each year, it feels special.

"I'm so grateful to be able to participate, I have tears in my eyes," she says. "I feel so blessed that I'm able to run. And I feel that's why I've been able to keep the cancer from coming back."

It was my way of dealing with cancer. If I could just stay in shape to do another marathon, then I knew I was okay.

CHERYL KARDISH-LEVITAN

SKIPPING THE RACE

Chris Baron of Oakville, Ontario skipped the entire marathon in an attempt to earn a spot in the Guinness Book of World Records. Baron skipped the race in a world record time of 4:49:39.5. "I tripped 17 times during the 42k which meant I had to stop, back up, complete two revolutions of the rope and get back to race pace immediately. The spectators were cheering louder than a stadium full of sports fans and would not let me stop...it was incredible," says Baron. He decided to attempt to break the record in Ottawa after the marathon he originally signed up for backed out a few weeks earlier. "I called up the (Ottawa) organizing committee, and in a 60-second elevator speech, sold them on the idea that they would see a world record on their turf if they'd give me the chance. History was made as family and friends traveled from abroad to the nation's capital on a beautiful sunny day to watch the record fall by more than 30 minutes."

HALF A MILLION REASONS

The 2005 Race Weekend raised $516,000 for the Ottawa Hospital Foundation. **Liz McGuire** was one of the runners who helped to generate funds. McGuire ran her first marathon in memory of her six-year-old niece Tanya Heney, who died of cancer in January 2004. McGuire says she started running again after Tanya was diagnosed. "It helped me get rid of some stress." McGuire continued to run and became an accomplished Masters athlete.

MOVING PICTURES

YouTube, the online video sharing and viewing community, was launched by Steve Chen, Chad Hurley, and Jawed Karim.

THE HONEYMOONERS

For many runners, finishing the marathon is a reason to celebrate. But for Winnipeg honeymooners Elaine and Cecil Embury, taking part in the Ottawa Race Weekend was the celebration. The couple decided to plan their wedding date for the week before the Ottawa Marathon, so they could marry, then travel to Ottawa for the honeymoon. Cecil did the half-marathon while Elaine ran the Ottawa Marathon for the first time.

NEW GG

Michaëlle Jean succeeded Adrienne Clarkson as Governor General of Canada.

2005

CANADIAN HERO

Steve Nash became the first Canadian-born player to be named the most valuable player in the NBA.

KENYANS ON TOP

At the 35-kilometre mark, Kenya's **David Cheruiyot** broke from the lead pack of six runners to capture the men's marathon in 2:14:20.3. Fellow Kenyan John Itati was second in 2:14:46.6, while Toronto's Danny Kassap placed third in his third career marathon in 2:15:12.6. Three-time champion Joseph Nderitu was fourth, and defending champion Elly Rono finished fifth.

FIRST UNDER NEW FLAG

Lidia Vasilevskaia of Russia was the first woman to cross the finish line in 2:31:52.7. She beat out Russian-born Lioudmila Kortchaguina of Toronto. But Kortchaguina didn't seem too disappointed by the second place finish. She received her Canadian citizenship just the week before, which meant it was her first race as a Canadian citizen. The second-place finish earned her the national women's marathon title for the first time.

FITS LIKE A GLOVE

Vibram, an Italian sole manufacturer, unveiled a prototype of their Five Fingers shoe, a glove-like slipper with individual toe compartments. The shoe debuted at the Boston Marathon in April the following year.

2006

Running to recover

4,217
marathon participants

+27c

2:12:18.2
Abderrahime Bouramdane
Men's Winner

2:29:42.1
Lioudmila Kortchaguina
Women's Winner

29,416
Race Weekend participants

In 2005, just over a year after he was seriously injured in a roadside attack in Afghanistan, Major Jay Feyko was posted to Ottawa.

"The first weekend that I was staying there happened to be the weekend of the Ottawa Marathon," he says. "I thought, this is perfect. I'm going to go down and watch some of it."

He soon discovered watching the race just wasn't enough.

"I thought, 'Why am I watching it?' I don't watch sports, I do sports.

"So as soon as I could, I registered for the marathon the next year. I did it before I was injured, so I can do it after I was injured."

Feyko's first marathon was in 1996. He and other members of the First Battalion Royal Canadian Regiment were training for an event called the Military Ironman. The race includes running, portaging and canoeing, all while wearing a 45-pound pack.

"As part of our training, we were all going to run the Ottawa Marathon," says Feyko.

Ottawa is typically warm in May, but on race day in 1996 there was heavy snow and a windchill factor of minus-8.

Even so, Feyko says, "It was a fantastic experience."

In 2003, Feyko was deployed to Afghanistan. A week before he was due to return from a six-month tour of duty, he was among a group of soldiers on patrol in Kabul when their vehicle was hit by a suicide bomber. Corporal Jamie Murphy was killed, and Feyko and two other soldiers were wounded.

The shrapnel from the bomb tore through Feyko's knee and shoulder, and he lost vision in his right eye. But he counts himself fortunate.

"It's just dumb luck that the shrapnel didn't hit me in different places," he says. "If I was sitting two centimetres to my right, I wouldn't be talking to you."

After a series of surgeries to remove the shrapnel, Feyko still found walking difficult, but he was determined to recover as fully as possible. He started playing hockey again. It was probably too soon, he says, but it was good for his mental health to be returning to an activity he enjoyed before he was wounded.

"I wanted to be as much the person I was after my injury as I was before my injury," he says.

He started running as part of his rehabilitation and, although it was painful at times, it became an important part of his recovery.

"If I got worked up about something, I'd just go for a run," he says. "That was my stress reliever. That was the mental aspect of my recovery. I can really think about things when I'm running."

Despite some chronic pain in his knee, the training for the 2006 marathon went well. "Ottawa is a beautiful city to run in," he says. "I had some very meaningful and patriotic runs."

This time, race day was very hot. Feyko struggled for part of the second half, but finished strongly.

About 500 metres from the finish line, a volunteer got his attention.

"She looked at my bib and got an excited expression on her face and started dialing a cell phone," he says. "Did I miss a turn? Did I screw up?

"She said, 'Are you Jay Feyko? You just won a car.'"

A local car dealer had provided a prize for the race and Feyko's name was chosen at random. By coincidence, he had just purchased a new vehicle the week before.

"That made for a fantastic finish," he says. "When am I ever going to run a marathon and win a car again?"

Winning a car was thrilling, but it was secondary to his main objective.

"I did it," says Feyko. "I ran only two marathons and they happened to be 10 years apart from each other. Now I can say I ran one after I was injured, just like before. It was very rewarding."

"When am I ever going to run a marathon and win a car again?

JAY FEYKO

TOO YOUNG TO RUN

India's **Budhia Singh**, known as the world's youngest marathon runner, was banned from long-distance running on humanitarian grounds. He was reported to have run 48 marathons by the age of four.

NEW CHAMPION

Five-time Paralympian **Jeff Adams** won the first official wheelchair marathon in a time of 1:33:48.4, the fastest time ever recorded in Canada.

THREE DECADES IN THE MAKING

It took 31 years, but Dr. Neil McGee finally completed his first full marathon. In 1975, McGee ran the first 13 kilometres of the very first Ottawa Marathon with his uncle Tim Hogan. McGee had intended to join his uncle for the first mile and ended up running almost a third of the race. But this time the emergency room physician trained to run the entire race and finished in 3:44:44.3. "I remember the last ten kilometers being very difficult," says McGee. He says he slowed down as the race passed through Vincent Massey Park, and struggled along Prince of Wales Drive. "I had never run this far, and my legs felt wooden as I ran through the Arboretum. But with the support of my family and the crowd lining the canal, I managed to cross the finish line. I had tears in my eyes as I completed my first marathon over 30 years after I first set out."

TOO BAD ABOUT THE MATH

Glenn Robertson was inspired to run because of two big milestones. "My marathon adventure was to convince myself that, although I had just retired and was turning 60, I wasn't over the hill just yet," he says. "I had trained pretty hard in the spring, so I felt I was in pretty good shape." The night before the marathon, he ran the 5k with his wife Diane and enjoyed the pasta dinner. On race day, he aimed for four hours. "My training was geared toward running 10k per hour, not realizing a marathon is more than 40k." So he finished in 4:20, "which was a little disappointing, but I guess not too bad for a 60-year-old who was running his first long-distance race."

EXCITED TO BE BEST

Toronto's Lioudmilla Kortchaguina broke the 22-year old course record as she won the women's race in 2:29:42. Her time was 55 seconds faster than the old record, set in 1984 by Sylvia Ruegger. "It's my personal best so I'm happy and I'm excited," Kortchaguina said after the race, draping a Maple Leaf flag around her shoulders at the finish line. The 2005 winner, Lidia Vasilevskaia, started the race, but dropped out due to injury. See her story in 2007.

UNFORTUNATE SHORTCUT

After a barricade was inadvertently moved, 14 runners shaved 400 metres off the course and had to be disqualified. Kenya's Amos Tirop Matui crossed the finish line first, but Abderrahime Bouramdane of Morocco was named the winner.

WII LIKE IT

Nintendo Wii was released on November 19, 2006, introducing a new form of player interaction to gaming.

BLONDE BOND

Daniel Craig appeared for the first time as James Bond in *Casino Royale*.

CALLING ON THE MOJO

At the age of 41, **Colleen Berry** finished her first marathon. "I hadn't run in any type of competition for over 22 years. This was just for the experience and to see what I could do," says Berry. "The heat was brutal. It was intimidating to see elites bonk, and I was inexperienced and not sure how I was going to finish. I relied on my mojo, Terry Fox, for inspiration and motivation to get through the final kilometres. To my surprise, I not only finished, but qualified for Boston."

REDEMPTION

Wayne Crowe's first Ottawa Marathon in 2005 didn't go as well as he had hoped. Because it was very warm, he says, "I faded badly in the second half. I came out of the hotel at 6 a.m. and felt warm in a singlet, even at that time of day. I was too inexperienced to recognize I should back off the pace, and paid for it," says Crowe. But the marathon in 2006 went more the way he hoped. He ran 2:55 to finish second in the men's 50-55 age group. For his running partner Steven Kilburn, the day went even better. Despite the heat he finished in 2:51 for a personal best.

TROY TO THE RESCUE

Janet Vanden Bosch of Edmonton was very grateful to a spectator she encountered 37 kilometres into a very hot race. "I ran into trouble and a bystander came to my rescue," Vanden Bosch wrote in a letter to the *Ottawa Citizen*. "A man I know only as Troy made it possible for me to complete the race. He helped me get running again, then came onto the course and ran with me for four kilometres to make sure I was okay. He also encouraged the spectators to cheer louder, helped other runners get aid, and was an all-around tremendous help." Vanden Bosch says he thanked the man, but "it didn't seem enough." She wrote, "Thanks Ottawa, you have a great marathon. Just make it a little cooler next year."

NEW PM

Stephen Harper became Canada's 22nd prime minister after the Conservative Party won the January election.

MAY

27

3,691
marathon participants

+14c

2:10:35.4
David Cheruiyot
Men's Winner

2:31:56.6
Lioudmila Kortchaguina
Women's Winner

30,468
Race Weekend participants

From Russia with speed

For Lioudmila Kortchaguina and her family, the Ottawa Marathon has become an annual tradition.

"We've lived in Canada 13 years," she says. "And I've only missed Ottawa Race Weekend twice. One was the first year, because I didn't know about it. The second time was because I was pregnant."

A big part of the tradition is Kortchaguina running with great success. Apart from 2008, when she withdrew at the last minute because of an injury, in her first seven trips to Ottawa she never finished lower than second place. She's the only four-time women's champion, winning in 2002, 2004, 2006 and 2007.

She was also the first woman to break 2:30 in Ottawa, setting a course record in 2006. And she was the Masters champion in the 10k in 2012 and in the marathon in 2013.

Kortchaguina says she has been running almost all her life. She was born in Russia and trained under the sophisticated and rigorous Soviet training system before moving to the Toronto area with her husband Ilia and daughter Polina in 2001.

"We knew Canada was a friendly, safe country," she says. "We decided to try it too and see what happens. We didn't have a lot of money and we didn't have the language. But that's the same as thousands of other people."

When they first arrived in their new home, the family's only source of income was Kortchaguina's prize money from running.

"It's my job and it's my love," she says. "It's what I can do and what I like to do. It doesn't matter where I am. I just need my running shoes and my running clothes. That's it."

Kortchaguina attributes her success and longevity in the sport to her training.

"It's all about hard work," she says. "The hard preparation for two or three months before the race. At the finish, especially if you finish first, the feeling is great. You can see that all you've done before has paid off for you at the finish line."

In 2005, having already won Ottawa twice, Kortchaguina achieved a special milestone. Two days before the marathon, she became a Canadian citizen.

"We got our citizenship on Friday," she says. "Friday afternoon we got in the car and drove to Ottawa. Sunday I won the Canadian championship. It all happened in about 44 hours. I was very proud."

She finished second in the race, but was the top Canadian. The next two years, she won both the race and the Canadian title. Kortchaguina has been the top Canadian five times in Ottawa, including in 2013.

"I always like to be in Ottawa," she says. "It's a very good place to run. This is the race I really love."

When the family started making the trip to Ottawa, Polina was four years old. Now she's 16 and has a younger brother who was born in 2011. In the past few years, Polina has volunteered at the race, helping out in the start and finish areas.

Over the dozen years she's been a regular presence in Ottawa, Kortchaguina has seen the event grow rapidly.

"It started as a regular, small race," she says. "Now it's huge, one of the biggest events in the world. So many people like to run Ottawa. It's incredible. It's a really good race. I love it."

THON
TAWA FINISH

:36:59

ING
1F CAN
Kortchaguina
CBC Radio-Canada

" So many
people like to
run Ottawa.
It's incredible.
It's a really
good race. I
love it. "

LIOUDMILA KORTCHAGUINA

I THINK I'LL SKIP IT THIS YEAR

Chris Baron of Oakville, Ontario returned to the Ottawa Marathon to try to eclipse his own Guinness World Record. And Baron succeeded, setting a new mark for skipping through a marathon, with a time of 4:28:49. He was joined by his father Al, a runner for more than 50 years, and his friends Karen and Stewart Paterson, who acted as his pace bunnies to ensure the run was authenticated for Guinness. "I got a hairline fracture at about 35k in my right ankle," he says. "I had to take my shoes off and finish the race barefoot. Ouch."

MILESTONE EVENT

Chris Burn of Peterborough, Ontario celebrated his 70th birthday by doing his first marathon. After a heart bypass in 2002, Burns and his wife Bodil took up running. "By 2007 I figured now or never," he says. With the help of his training partner, Arlene Blunck, Burn finished in just three seconds less than eight hours.

FIRST AMONG FIRSTS

Kenyan runner **David Cheruiyot** broke the course record, finishing in 2:10:35. The previous course record of 2:11:47 was set in 2004 by Elly Rono, also from Kenya. "I came back to Ottawa this year because it is a great race," Cheruiyot told the *Ottawa Citizen*. "It was hard because there's many guys, very strong guys." The defending champion, Abderrahime Bouramdane, was one of those strong competitors. He was right on Cheruiyot's heels, crossing the finish line just five seconds later.

TOUCH THIS

The first generation of the iPhone was released on June 29, 2007.

IT'S ABOUT TIME

Greg Billingham finished the London Marathon one week after the event started. The 39-year-old moved through the marathon at an ultra-slow pace of less than half a kilometre per hour to raise money for charity.

RUNNING ON FAMILIAR GROUND

Former Carleton University student **Suzanne Evans** made the trek back to Ottawa from New Westminster, B.C. to run the race for the first time. And the cheering section that came out to support her made it well worth the journey. Evans's sister and her family, as well as her parents, who made the drive from Hudson, Quebec, were all there to see Evans come in second in the women's 35 to 39 category. "Being out here on the West Coast, it's not often I have such a cheering squad along the way and at the finish!" It was so much fun, Evans came back the next year.

HEY, ISN'T THAT...

Gatineau's **Giorgio Vecco** had a good story to tell after running his first and only marathon. As he was running along the Rideau Canal near the 15-kilometre checkpoint, he saw a face he recognized right away. It was former prime minister Jean Chretien, standing outside his home. "I think he was picking up the newspaper," says Vecco. "I yelled, 'Hello Mr. Chretien!' and he yelled 'Hello!' back and waved."

INDIE WINNER

Juno won the Academy Award for Best Original Screenplay and earned three other Oscar nominations, including Best Picture, and Best Actress for Canadian-born Ellen Page.

2007

"A big thank you to all the volunteers and cheerers for the Ottawa Marathon on Sunday. As one of the runners who wasn't in the front of the pack or even the middle, it was really nice to still have people out cheering, especially in the rain, as I made my way around the course. The volunteers at the water stations and road barriers and the musicians were great and very supportive. They all helped me achieve my goal of finishing a marathon."

Jane Scott, in a letter to the *Ottawa Citizen*.

A healthy addiction

MAY 25

4,019
marathon participants

+20c

2:10:59.8
David Cheruiyot
Men's Winner

2:28:43.9
Asmae Leghzaoui
Women's Winner

32,970
Race Weekend participants

Every runner follows the same route to the finish line of a marathon. But not everyone follows an identical path to the start.

In 2008, a small group of runners turned off a dangerous road of alcohol, drugs, and, in some cases, crime, and aimed themselves toward the Ottawa Marathon. The eight men were all connected to Harvest House, a residential treatment program in Ottawa.

Coached by Phil Marsh of the Running Room, the runners replaced a harmful addiction with a healthy one, replacing drugs and alcohol with hard training for their first marathon. And every one of them crossed the finish line.

Using drugs from the age of 12, David Gagnon dropped out of high school. Before going to Harvest House, he was using cocaine heavily. As part of his recovery, he joined the running program, and completed the 10k at Ottawa Race Weekend in 2007. But training for the marathon the next year required much more effort.

"It was quite the crazy experience," he says. "The marathon was a whole different ballgame. You're training almost every day instead of a couple of times a week."

Before entering Harvest House, Joshua Hambleton had hit a series of lows in school and work. "I was pretty messed up," he says.

But by the time the marathon training started, he had graduated from the residential program and was back in school. He had even recently completed his first triathlon. The staff at Harvest House asked him to join the running group as a mentor.

The training was not easy. Both Hambleton and Gagnon remember long training runs on harsh winter days in January.

"One time we were running in a blizzard," says Hambleton. "I remember ice pellets hitting our faces," says Gagnon.

Gagnon says he remembers that some of the other residents at Harvest House would come outside to cheer the runners when they got back from their training runs. For him, the training created as much benefit as the marathon itself.

"It helped focus your mind on something good instead of thinking of something bad," he says. "Seeing you're able to accomplish something that you weren't able to accomplish before. It's a different kind of rush.

And also, we started to have a good, healthy lifestyle. We were eating properly. We were going to bed at a good time. It helped me stop smoking. All that put together was a clean change for us."

"For me, it was about structured goal attainment," says Hambleton. "Sometimes we have a sense of entitlement and we believe life should be easy for us. One of the things the training taught me was the structure of laying the groundwork and being diligent in those early months to build up those kilometres. It paid off on race day.

"You train for battle, and on the day of battle, things go your way. That was one of the most valuable lessons."

On race day, the runners stayed together for the first half of the course. Hambleton says he surprised himself when he decided to abandon his own goals and stick with one of the other runners, to support him all the way through to the finish.

"I remember pulling him along, deciding that my time didn't matter," he says. "It became more about us finishing together. So that was a different experience for me. But I remember the satisfaction of having someone depend on me. That was one of the things it taught me."

Gagnon has run a total of four marathons. Now 25, he's been sober for seven-and-a-half years. Both he and Hambleton say their greatest satisfaction came from seeing the other runners, from the group finish the race.

"It was very important that everybody finish," Gagnon says. "We started as a team, and we finished as a team."

"For me, it was just keeping my word," says Hambleton. "I said that I would do it. There wasn't a lot of intrinsic motivation for me. But I got a lot of satisfaction from seeing everyone at the finish line."

"
You train for battle, and on the day of battle, things go your way. That was one of the most valuable lessons. "

JOSHUA HAMBLETON

RUNNING TOWARD RECOVERY

As the medical director for the event, **Jon Hooper** was used to helping runners recover after the Ottawa Marathon. But in 2008, Hooper was able to see his own wife among the runners who crossed the finish line. **Sindy Hooper** ran her first marathon in 2008, qualifying for Boston. She went on to qualify for Boston every year after. In January 2013, Sindy was diagnosed with pancreatic cancer. Despite her symptoms and the fact that she was undergoing chemotherapy, she continued to run, using it as a way to raise awareness of the disease and money for Pancreatic Cancer Canada.

STARTING YOUNG

Hundreds of youngsters ran the new kids' marathon that was added to Ottawa Race Weekend.

SURPRISE HIT

Slumdog Millionaire was the sleeper hit movie of the year. The film won eight Academy Awards, the most for any film in 2008, including Best Picture, Best Director, and Best Adapted Screenplay.

HISTORIC MOMENT

Barack Obama was elected the 44th president of the United States.

BIO SHOE

Brooks introduced BioMoGo, the world's first biodegradable midsole.

A BOUNCE FROM FLAT COKE

Ever since he was in high school, **Eric Emery** wanted to run a marathon. In 2008, Emery finally made it to the start line. "I was so excited at the start when Frank Shorter, the famous American marathoner in the 1970s, gave a pre-race speech. I remember him running the 1976 Olympic marathon in Montreal," says Emery. He remembers Shorter saying that he used to drink flat Coke during marathons, and advising runners not to go out too fast and to be prepared for the final 10k. "He was so right. The 30k mark came and went with not too much difficulty, but I remember the final 10k being a real struggle just to hang on. To help me along, my dad came out to give me Frank Shorter's recipe of flat Coke. The feeling at the finish line was unbelievable. I finally did it!"

ONE FOR THE AGES

Ottawa's **Paula Hickman** broke the record for Canadian women aged 55-59. In only her second marathon, the 57-year-old Hickman finished in 3:11:34.7, beating the previous record set by Diane Palmason in 1993. But the record isn't the only memory that stood out for Hickman. "One thing I do remember about that marathon was running through the water station in Rockcliffe," says Hickman. "All the young volunteers were lined up high-fiving everyone. It was so cool – a very fun moment during the rigours of a marathon. And of course, crossing the finish line knowing I had got the record was special, although I badly wanted to sit down, and went straight to the medical tent."

2008

TEARS OF JOY, NOT PAIN

Vida Barker says she will always remember her first marathon. "I had just run my first half-marathon in March, so it was an ambitious plan to train for the Ottawa Marathon just two months later. My good friend and fellow runner Charlene convinced me, and we trained together, but unfortunately she was injured and couldn't run with me." But Charlene still travelled to Ottawa with Barker and a group of runners from Pickering, cheered them on at the start of the race, met them at the halfway point to re-stock their gels, and ran with Barker for the last few kilometers. "Just handing off my waterbelt to her at 38k gave me the extra energy I needed to finish strong," says Barker. Her daughter Allison lived in Ottawa and was working as a volunteer at the finish line. "I gave her a big hug and was crying; she was so worried that I was injured – but they were tears of joy."

A REASON TO SMILE

In 2006, **Daniel Bingham** of Waterloo came up with a list of 99 things he wanted to accomplish in life. Number three on that list was to run a marathon. In May 2008, he did it. "What amazes me is how joyful the race was," he says. "I think I must have been smiling for the majority of the run, breaking out into a huge grin on many an occasion. What a gift." Bingham says he was very thankful to the city and people of Ottawa. "You can't truly understand what it's like until you've done it, to be cheered on by the smiles and clapping of thousands of people who have come out of their homes to see you through. The race involves a lot of work, and the dedicated volunteers are out there filling cups, cleaning up the big mess, and doing whatever they can to make it a great experience for the runners. Volunteers rock!"

4,163

marathon participants

☉+18c

2:13:22.6

David Cheruiyot

Men's Winner

2:27:40.9

Asmae Leghzaoui

Women's Winner

36,694

Race Weekend participants

A is for amazing

At the end of a long journey, it's always good to come home. When Gavin Lumsden ran the Ottawa Marathon in 2009, he wasn't returning from a recent trip. But Ottawa was the last leg of an arduous four-year quest that involved travelling to marathons thousands of miles from home.

Inspired by fitness advocate Sean Egan, who died in an attempt to climb Mount Everest in 2005, Lumsden set out to raise awareness and money to fight childhood obesity.

"He convinced me we would be in a world of trouble if we didn't do something about the trend," he says.

Lumsden began by helping to establish a couple of fitness programs for children in Ottawa. But when one program went on hiatus because of a lack of funding, he decided more had to be done. And while running a marathon in Cumberland, just east of Ottawa, an idea struck him.

"I'd already done Amsterdam and Berlin," he said. "Here I was in Cumberland. That's A, B and C. What would it be like to finish the alphabet? That was how it started."

Lumsden decided to complete 26 marathons covering every letter from A to Z. The first step was to determine whether there actually were a marathon corresponding to each letter of the alphabet. He started researching trips to North American destinations like Edmonton, Winnipeg, Philadelphia, and Miami and European spots like Rome, Inverness (in Scotland), and Flanders (in Belgium).

"At first it seemed pie-in-the-sky," he says. "But the more I researched it, the more it seemed I could pull it off."

For more obscure letters, he found marathons in places like Ucluelet, British Columbia and Yonkers, New York.

"The big one was X," he says. "That could have led to a trip to China that would have cost me $6,000 to $8,000. But a friend of mine spotted this marathon in Xenia, Ohio. That was a lot more economically feasible."

Over the course of the next four years, he started ticking off the marathons, sometimes leaving work at 6:00 on a Friday evening, flying to another city, running a marathon Sunday morning, flying home, and arriving for work Monday morning.

He saved his hometown marathon for last. Lumsden leads an annual marathon clinic at the Running Room, so he's passionate about the Ottawa Marathon.

"There is only one experience that trumps the feeling of joy and euphoria of crossing the finish line of your first marathon, and that's to witness somebody else doing exactly that," he says. "I've stood at the finish line for four hours and watched people cross. It's so uplifting to see people achieve their goals and do something they probably never imagined they would."

For his final race, he recruited 40 friends to run with him and raise money for an endowment to address the financial obstacles that get in the way of healthy activities for some children.

"The biggest challenge is for kids that are from difficult circumstances and can't afford to join the Y or pay for other fitness programs," he says. "Together, as a group, we raised $29,000 which sits at the Y as an endowment so that underprivileged kids who want to join the program can do so."

On race day, Lumsden wanted the entire group to cross the finish line together, so he arranged for everyone to meet at a specific time near the finish line. But he fell behind when he encountered a friend who was struggling on the course and ran with him for a few kilometres.

"I looked at my watch and thought, 'Yikes! If I don't get moving I'm not going to make it on time.' I'm sure I ran the next 4k in probably the fastest I've ever done."

At the finish line, the group crossed together, wearing matching t-shirts. Someone presented Lumsden with the 25 medals from his previous marathons, and he put all of them around his neck, along with the new one from Ottawa. "That must have weighed 40 pounds," he says.

Lumsden says the Ottawa Marathon, the last of his 26, went by more quickly than any other.

"I was excited to be finishing something I'd been working for four years," he says.

It's so uplifting to see people achieve their goals and do something they probably never imagined they would.

GAVIN LUMSDEN

FIRE IN THE HOUSE

On its way to Vancouver in 2010, the Olympic torch arrived at Parliament Hill and was carried into the House of Commons by Olympic figure skating champion **Barbara Ann Scott**.

DEJA VU

For the first time in the race's history, both the top female and top male runners were repeat winners. Kenya's **David Cheruiyot** and **Asmae Leghzaoui** of Morocco were the champions for the second year in the row. Cheruiyot also became the first man to win the race four times.

JUST LIKE DAD

Pierre Laporte ran his ninth marathon, and his fastest, in 3:47. His daughter Stella Ray greeted him at the finish. "That was by far the best marathon because I inspired my little girl to become a runner like her dad," He says Stella Ray ran the 2k at Ottawa Race Weekend in 2011.

SOCK NEWS

Swiss company SIGVARIS launches a new line of compression socks for sports, including running. Marathoner Paula Radcliffe had been wearing them for years.

COVERING THE WEEKEND

The Arnotts of the Toronto area made Ottawa Race Weekend a family affair. Among them, they participated in all the events in 2009. Colin Arnott was the 3:30 pace bunny for the marathon, pacing his wife Lee Anne. His brother Ken was the 1:35 pace bunny for the half-marathon. Sister Sharon ran the 10k, and father Gord and Colin's son Carey each ran the 5k. Lee Anne ran a personal best of 3:32. "She tried to stay with me, but fell off with about 5k to go," says Colin. "We got all pumped up the night before the marathon, watching my dad, sister, and son run the 5 and 10k".

2009

HAPPY ANNIVERSARY

Denise Huneault and her husband Michel Villeneuve of St-Jérôme, Quebec ran the marathon to celebrate their 25th wedding anniversary. It was Denise's third marathon and Michel's 49th. Denise had not run a marathon since 1996, and says she was pleasantly surprised by the results.

LOVING OTTAWA

Running partners **Louanna Bethune** and **Annette Love** of Halifax crossed the line hand-in-hand to finish their first ever marathon. "I had previously run two Ottawa half-marathons, and wanted my first full to be there, as I love the event," says Bethune. Between them, the pair has since run 14 marathons – five for Bethune and nine for Love. "We both attribute Ottawa for giving us the running bug, which is evident in the look on our faces."

THE KING OF POP IS DEAD

Superstar **Michael Jackson** died at the age 50.

RHYTHM SECTION

The Ottawa Drum Club brought a little music to the 2009 marathon. One of many forms of entertainment along the route, the club played from the time the lead runners passed by at about 7:30 a.m. until the last runner arrived at 11:15. "Runners like us because they can hear us from almost one kilometre away," says drum club member Charles St-Jean. The eight members in the band have known each other since they were 15, and were still playing together at sixty. They made their first appearance at the marathon in 2009, and have played every year since.

One world record after another

🌡+16c

2:09:33.4
Arata Fujiwara
Men's Winner

2:28:19.0
Merima Mohammed
Women's Winner

39,010
Race Weekend participants

When Rick Ball wanted to break his own world record in the marathon in 2010, he decided Ottawa was the perfect place to do it.

"There are so many reasons," says Ball. "It's the nation's capital. It's scenic. And it's the crowd support. A lot of marathons just don't have that many people cheering you on. You need that when you're running a marathon."

Only three years earlier, Ball wasn't even a runner. He lost a leg in a devastating motorcycle accident in 1986, and although he took up other sports like cycling and cross-country skiing, he was never able to find a prosthetic leg that didn't cause painful blisters when he tried to run.

In 2007, he tried a new artificial leg that was much more comfortable. "Then I discovered I have this natural talent," he says.

Ball had never done much running before he lost his leg. But wh en he started running with his new prosthetic leg, he learned he was pretty fast. And being able to run quickly changed his life.

"It made me feel whole again," he says. "When I'm running, I don't even think of the leg. It's like I'm totally able-bodied again."

Ball set a goal of qualifying for the Boston Marathon. He could have entered as an athlete with a disability, but he was so fast he made the qualifying time for able-bodied men his age.

In Boston in 2009, he decided to go for the world record for single-leg amputees. He ran 3:01:50, two minutes faster than the previous standard.

Just a few weeks later, Ball set a new 10k record in Ottawa. He went on to break the half-marathon record that fall.

Just two years into his running career, he had set three world records in one year. Breaking records, he says, became almost like an addiction. He kept asking himself, "What's next?"

The marathon, he decided, still represented some unfinished business. Ball decided he wanted to be the first single-leg amputee to break three hours. So he signed up for Ottawa.

On race day, the conditions were ideal for Ball. He ran the first half in about one hour and 27 minutes, leaving himself a cushion for the second half. In the final few kilometres, he knew his goal was within reach.

"I was feeling the pain, but I knew that I was going to do it," he says. "It was mental at that point."

Ball finished in 2:57. The crowd, he says, was crucial to his success.

"It's a big factor when you're trying for a record," he says. "When you start feeling the pain, and you don't think you'll be able to go any further, that's when you need the crowd support, and there's huge crowd support in Ottawa.

"Everybody knew I was going for the record. They were really supportive. That's a big factor when you're going for a record."

Ball says he'll always remember the moment he reached the finish line.

"Everybody was roaring," he says. "It was an amazing feeling to cross that finish line to accomplish that ultimate goal."

After breaking his own world record, Ball started training in shorter distances, and eventually represented Canada at the Para Pan Am games in 2011. He's suffered a few injuries along the way, but his goal is to continue running competitively for as long as he can.

No matter what happens, the Ottawa Marathon in 2010 will always be one of the highlights of his running career and his life.

"I didn't realize it at the time, but that was the last marathon I ran," he says. "I never ran another one. But I'm satisfied. I feel like I accomplished everything I can in the marathon."

FINISH

2:57:47
TIMEX

TIMEX

BALL

"When I'm running,
I don't even think of the leg.
It's like I'm totally
able-bodied again.

RICK BALL

CANADIAN CHAMP

Krista DuChene placed sixth overall in the women's division and won the Canadian title. Competing under ideal weather conditions, with overcast skies and cool temperatures, 33-year-old DuChene finished her fourth marathon in 13 months in 2:39:07.3. It was her first national title.

NEW COURSE RECORD

Japan's **Arata Fujiwara** became the first runner to break 2:10 in Ottawa and set the men's course record with a time of 2:09:33. It was his first marathon win.

BITTERSWEET WIN

Stephen Drew of Kitchener, Onatrio was the first Canadian men's finisher in the marathon, with a time of 2:21:46.3. Afterward, the one-time Ottawa resident broke down in tears thinking about his longtime coach, Terry Goodenough, who wasn't there to see it. Drew told the *Ottawa Citizen*, "I wish he were here to see this."

42.2 FOR FORTY

In May 2010, **Audrey Taylor** turned 40 and decided the best gift she could give herself would be the satisfaction of completing a marathon. She finished in 4 hours and 17 minutes, using her first marathon to raise money for Canadian Breast Cancer Foundation. "I got lots of support before and during the race," says Taylor. "And of course, a great sense of achievement once I crossed the finish line."

VICE-REGAL RUNNER

David Johnston is sworn in as the 28th Governor General of Canada.

TABLET ARRIVES

The first iPad hit the market.

LAYTON'S BATTLE

New Democratic Party Leader Jack Layton announced that he had prostate cancer.

2010

COMEBACK TRAIL

Mary Davies was a competitive field hockey player in New Zealand who stumbled into long-distance running. She turned out to be a natural, but almost had to give it up after contracting mono in 2009. A year-and-a-half later, she was back running, in her first Ottawa marathon. Davies finished the 2010 race as the 27th woman overall, and first in her age category with a time of 2:39:29.6. She ran the Ottawa Marathon again in 2012, and won the Scotiabank Toronto Waterfront Marathon that fall.

BIGFOOT ON THE BEACH

Ottawa's **Mark Newman** completed his first full marathon after his wife signed him up for the event while they were travelling around Asia. The couple was on a six-month trip with their two children when Newman started running on the beaches of Goa and Thailand. "I didn't have any running shoes to start training in. It turns out size 12 running shoes are not a usually stocked size in Malaysia! I had to settle for a size 11, and, as a result, sacrificed two toenails," he remembers. "I did enjoy running on the beaches in the heat, and have fond memories of the kids coming out with water or fruit at various times to keep me going."

RUN FOR GRANNIES

Seventy-year-old **Bodil Burn** ran her first marathon to celebrate turning 70. The retired bus driver from Peterborough, Ontario came first in her age category. Burn was following in the footsteps of her husband Chris. He walked the course in 2007, when he turned 70, and again in 2008 and 2012. Bodil Burn grew up in Kenya, and used her marathon, training to raise about $2,700 for African grandmothers caring for children orphaned by AIDS. According to her husband, after completing the marathon, Bodil Burn swore she would never do another one.

GOLD FOR CANADA

Canadian **Alexandre Bilodeau** became the first Canadian to win an Olympic gold medal on Canadian soil at the Vancouver Olympics. Canada won 14 gold, the most ever captured by one country at a Winter Games.

2011

A new set of eyes

5,087
marathon participants

🌡️+18c

2:10:17.9
Laban Moiben
Men's Winner

2:32:14.0
Kebebush Haile Lema
Women's Winner

39,992
Race Weekend participants

For most people, running is an individual sport. But other than on a treadmill, Ron Hackett cannot run alone. To complete a marathon – as Hackett has done 16 times – he needs a little help.

In 1966, when he was 11 years old, Hackett was a passenger in a vehicle that was struck head-on by a drunk driver. He lost almost all of his vision. What little he had left – seeing the occasional bright light – eventually disappeared.

As an adult, Hackett started running in an attempt to address his painful arthritic knees. He first tried swimming to relieve the discomfort, but that didn't help.

"I started doing gym classes," he says, "but that was awkward because I couldn't see what the instructor was doing."

Someone he met at the gym suggested Hackett try running. Before long, his knees started improving, and he was training for a half-marathon.

"I found the more I did it, the better it felt," he says. "I have absolutely no knee troubles now. I really attribute it to all the running I did and still do."

That first half-marathon, which he ran with the help of a guide, was "very, very slow," he says. But he was proud to finish it and he was soon training for the Ottawa Marathon in 1989.

"It was a real thrill finishing that," he says. It was his first of a dozen Ottawa Marathons.

Over the years, Hackett has finished races with several different guides. He runs regularly on the treadmill, but he's also done a few training runs while holding a rope tied to the bumper of his girlfriend's car.

Hackett has kept up his running through a series of health scares, including a brain abscess and prostate cancer. Being able to run, he says, has been a great liberator.

"Running is a must," he says. "It's a great stress reliever. It's as good for the mind as it is for the body.

"Problems always seem a little bit smaller at the end of a run. If I don't get anything done but I get my run in, then it wasn't a total waste of a day."

In 2010, Hackett decided to try qualifying for the Boston Marathon. Just a few days before a qualifying race in Picton, Ontario, he hooked up with Tim Scapillato, a runner from Gatineau who responded to a request for a guide on Facebook.

The night before the race, Hackett met Scapillato for the first time.

"We went for a 10-minute run through his neighbourhood and he taught me how to guide him," says Scapillato. "The next day we ran the race, and he qualified for Boston."

Together, Hackett and Scapillato completed both Boston and Ottawa in 2011, 2012, and 2013, with Hackett turning in some of the fastest times of his life. When they run together, Hackett puts his arm on Scapillato's elbow and the two run in stride. Hackett sets the pace, and Scapillato gives him quick instructions if there are obstacles or changes in the course ahead.

"It's been a great experience," says Scapillato. "Being the set of eyes for someone else has given me a whole new perspective on running."

Scapillato says one of the first things he noticed is how much spectators respond to a visually impaired runner.

"It's amazing," he says. "The crowds just go nuts when they see the two of you. I've run Ottawa so many times, but doing it with Ron was like running it again for the first time. It's so amazing to be cheered on from start to finish."

"I love Ottawa," says Hackett. "It's an interesting course, it's well-organized, and it's well-supported. It's a great marathon."

"Running is a must. It's a great stress reliever. It's as good for the mind as it is for the body."

RON HACKETT

COLD CASH

In November 2011, the Bank of Canada introduced polymer banknotes for the $100 bill, to modernize the currency and reduce counterfeiting.

THIRD TIME LUCKY

The men's and women's champions each won Ottawa in their third attempt. Kenya's **Laban Moiben** won the men's title in 2:10:17.9, and **Kebebush Haile Lema** of Ethiopia was the top female in 2:32:14.0. Moiben was a runner-up in 2010, and came fourth in 2009. Lema was second in 2007, and third in 2008.

A COURSE FOR ADVENTURE

The marathon adopted a new route that passed through communities such as Chinatown, Little Italy, and Westboro. **Richard Borsos** (bib number 4938) says he loved running through the city's different neighbourhoods. Borsos says Hintonburg had the loudest crowd support outside of the finish area. He also enjoyed passing important Ottawa sites such as Rideau Hall, the residence of the Governor General, who came out to cheer runners on. "Thank you, David Johnston, for standing at the side of the road and giving high fives," says Borsos.

RUNNING FOR THE FAMILY

Benard Onsare finished sixth in the 2011 Ottawa Marathon. A native of Kenya, Onsare was one of a number of runners who moved to Canada in order to race and earn money for his family at home. Onsare didn't own a pair of running shoes until he was 17 years old.

HAND-IN-HAND

It was an emotional race for **Christelle Desgranges-Farquhar**. Her mother and sister Delphine flew to Ottawa from Paris so that the two sisters could run the marathon together in memory of their father Gérard Desgranges, who passed away six months earlier from cancer. Desgranges-Farquhar remembers the race as rainy and gruelling, but the sisters finished hand-in-hand. "It was a beautiful experience for the two of us," she says. "I think my sister fell in love with Ottawa that day."

COMEBACK SID

After missing almost a year of hockey because of concussion symptoms, **Sidney Crosby** returned to the ice on November 21, 2011, scoring two goals and adding two assists against the New York Islanders.

2011

2012

5,290
marathon participants

🌡+14c

2:09:12.9
Laban Moiben
Men's Winner

2:28:45.9
Yeshi Esayias
Women's Winner

42,573
Race Weekend participants

Thirty and counting

When Daniel Fricker was a young father, the only time he got a workout was when he was doing household chores.

"My exercise was principally mowing the lawn," he says.

Fricker ran cross-country in high school and university, and competed in other sports, including wrestling, during his military service.

But after a long break from sports, Fricker decided in his mid-40s that he needed to get in better shape. So he took advantage of an offer from his employer to extend his lunch break by 30 minutes if he signed up for an exercise program.

At first, he swam a mile every day. But when a colleague suggested he take up running, it launched him on a marathon career that has spanned three decades. Fricker started running 10 kilometres every lunch hour and doing longer runs on the weekend from his home in Quebec's Eastern Townships.

"One thing led to another, and eventually I ended up saying I'd like to try running a marathon," he says.

His colleague had run Ottawa the year before, and told Fricker it was a great race. So Fricker travelled to the capital and ran his first marathon in 1983.

"I liked it, so I kept on doing it," says Fricker.

He kept on doing it every year without interruption. In 2012, Fricker completed the Ottawa Marathon for the 30th year in a row.

He's now finished more than 90 marathons. And along the way he inspired his wife, Yolande Marois, to join him. Marois started running when she was 60.

"It became a tradition for me and my wife to go to Ottawa every spring," says Fricker.

"Ottawa's a fabulous town. It's a very delightful city to visit."

Marois is 10 years older than her husband. "I like to say she stole me out of my mother's baby carriage," Fricker says.

Together, the couple travelled to Ottawa and other destinations to enter races. Fricker has finished the New York City Marathon 17 times, and Marois joined him on several occasions. In both 2008 and 2009, Marois received a special award from New York officials for being the oldest woman to complete the race.

Marois took a break from marathons after completing more than 20 of them. But she continued to join her husband most years on his spring trip to Ottawa, doing the half-marathon while he participated in the marathon.

Fricker says his wife recently started talking about doing another marathon. She just turned 89.

Fricker says he enjoys the ambiance of the Ottawa race. "It has a great feeling," he says. "The people, the staff and everything are always very welcoming and friendly. And during the marathon itself, you run with people – unknown people – and it's always very congenial."

And the marathon still appeals to Fricker at 78 years of age. "It's a never-ending objective," he says.

But even though he's getting close to completing 100 marathons, he's not motivated by milestones.

"I've never been trying to achieve a number objective," he says. "What happens, happens. As age advances, you never know when you might not be doing marathons anymore."

After a pause and a chuckle, he adds, "Or anything at all."

"The people, the staff and everything are always very welcoming and friendly.

DANIEL FRICKER

RUNNER'S HIGH

After training at altitude for three months, Ethiopia's **Yeshi Esayias** won the women's marathon by almost four-and-a-half minutes, in a time of 2:28:45.9

SUPPORT AROUND EVERY CORNER

Laila Nabizada of Montreal started running in 2008, and decided to make Ottawa her first marathon. She wasn't disappointed with the experience. "In every single corner, you had families standing in front of their doors, on the street, around the Rideau Canal to cheer us," she says. After a while, Nabizada noticed a couple on their bicycles who were following the same route as her. "I made a joke with them, saying that they were following me," she says. "I chose them as my own supporters. They followed me in each angle of the city, and I was so blessed by their presence that I was pushed till the end. I would like to thank them from the bottom of my heart."

FLIPPED FOR IT

The 2012 Summer Olympics were held in London. More than 10,000 athletes from 205 countries participated in the Games. Trampoline gymnast **Rosie MacLennan** was the only Canadian to win a gold medal. Canada also won five silver and 12 bronze medals.

FASTEST EVER

Kenyan **Laban Moiben** broke the course record in a time of 2:09:12, shaving 19 seconds off the previous time set in 2009.

2012

RELAY RACE

After the race, Jim Robinson retired, and **John Halvorsen (right)**, the past course record holder in the 10k, took over as race director.

PENNY DROPPED

Just a few weeks before the marathon, the Royal Canadian Mint manufactured its last penny.

LESSON LEARNED

Running his first marathon, **Mike Hogan** remembers feeling pretty good at 18k, "which was probably not a good thing," he says. "We closed the gap on the pace bunny, and quietly overtook him. In hindsight, passing a running expert, not even half way in, while running your first ever marathon sounds a bit stupid. Lesson learned." Hogan says the next 24 kilometres were a lot harder. But he finished in 4:14. "There were no fist pumps, nor smiles, but I did manage a few halfhearted victory signs for the camera."

SHOE IN

For some people, simply running a gruelling 42 kilometres isn't enough of a challenge. Soleman, otherwise known as **Geordie McConnell**, ran the entire 2012 marathon in a giant shoe costume. He wore the carefully designed aparatus for a good cause – to raise money for Sole Responsibility, a charity that collects shoes for Africa. But McConnell says he also just wanted to "bring more fun to the Ottawa Marathon."

GETTING IT RIGHT

In 2010, **Brian Letourneau** attempted his first Ottawa Marathon and had to stop at 41k because of dehydration, ending up in the medical tent. In 2011, he tried again, but started out too fast and "bonked" at 32k. "In 2012, I got it right and completed the marathon," he says. The next year, he served as a pace bunny. "Guess I figured I wouldn't screw up and go too fast," he says.

GREY MATTERS

Fifty Shades of Grey became the fastest-selling paperback book of all time.

2013

MAY 26

6,262
marathon participants

🌡 **+16c**

2:08:04.8
Tariku Jufar
Men's Winner

2:25:30.1
Yeshi Esayias
Women's Winner

44,123
Race Weekend participants

Running for her life

There are two Silvie Michauds. There's the one who was a heavy smoker, weighed 250 pounds, and had high blood pressure. And there's the one who runs marathons. And one doesn't even recognize the other.

"I don't remember who I was before," says Michaud. "I didn't realize you could change that much."

In 2004, Michaud's knees hurt, and she had trouble breathing when she went for a walk. She decided to do something about it. So she quit smoking and started walking more often.

"But then walking wasn't enough anymore," she says. "I would actually dream at night that I was running. I loved running when I was a kid. I guess I had totally forgotten about that. It was 'way back in my mind, really deep."

Michaud started running for 30 seconds and walking for one minute. She ran at night so that no one could see what she was doing. And she says that, at the outset, she had to overcome a bit of fear of the unknown.

"I thought I was too old to begin running," she says. "People scare you to death. They say it's not good for you, it's bad for your knees and back. But I wanted a better life for myself."

Eventually she was running 10 minutes without stopping, then 20. Within a year she had lost 85 pounds. Her blood pressure was down and she felt years younger. She started being more careful about what she ate.

"Running was making me really happy," she says. "It became a habit. So I wanted to run more and more and see where it would get me."

She began thinking about completing a marathon, and started running longer distances. She discovered she enjoyed the commitment required to follow a training plan.

"I love the discipline," she says. "Discipline is what we're missing these days in society. We forgot how happiness comes from effort."

She finished her first marathon in Montreal in 2009.

"Oh my God, did it hurt," she says. "But oh my God, was I happy. It's up there with giving birth to my son. That's how I felt when I crossed the finish line. I think I cried for half an hour."

She has since run five more, including Ottawa in 2013. "I loved it," she says. "To this day, its my favourite one. The route is amazing. There were people everywhere. The crowd was incredible."

Michaud plans to do many more marathons, as much for the training as the race itself.

"I look forward to every run," she says. "I was a great beginner but I had a hard time finishing stuff. Training for marathons changed that. Now I finish what I begin."

Running has even led Michaud to a new career as a personal trainer. As far as she's concerned, since she started running, she has become an entirely new person.

"Are you kidding me? I would never put a cigarette in my mouth," she says. "Running has made me a better person altogether.

"I tell people if you could be in my body now and inside my body before, you would understand why I'm so passionate about it," she says. "I can't believe I lived that long without it. I'm going to run until I have no legs."

> # I wanted to run more and more and see where it would get me.
>
> **SYVLIE MICHAUD**

LEARNING OPPORTUNITY

"Maybe it's the proximity of my home to the start line, maybe it's my familiarity with the course route and some of the spectators lining it, maybe it's the climate in late May, or maybe it's because twice now I have run it some five weeks after Boston, but after all three of my Ottawa marathons I am more compelled than usual to examine my training, my potential, and my race acumen. I have found I learn more about myself from this marathon than any other, making it a not-to-be-missed opportunity, each year it presents itself."

DIANA BABOR

FUTURE KING

Prince George of Cambridge was born July 22, 2013 to the Duke and Duchess of Cambridge, becoming third in line to the throne.

AT LAST, RECORD FALLS

Lanni Marchant of London, Ontario finished the Toronto Waterfront Marathon in 2:28:00, just over a half-minute ahead of Krista DuChene of Brantford, Ontario, who clocked a race time of 2:28:32. Both times beat Sylvia Ruegger's previous Canadian marathon record of 2:28:36, which had been set in Houston in 1985.

STANDOUT RACE

The Ottawa Marathon stood out among the 28 that Québec City's **Denis Lefebvre** has completed, he says, because of the weather, his running partners, his family supporters, and a general good feeling while he was running. "Given all those best conditions, guess what happened? I ran my PB, 3:11:21.5, and finished first in my category," says the 63-year-old. "I never thought that I could record a new PB. And I will always remember all the feelings and emotions that struck me when crossing the finish line."

BOSTON STRONG

After the shocking bombings at the finish line of the Boston Marathon in April, many runners wore special t-shirts in Ottawa to honour and raise money for the victims.

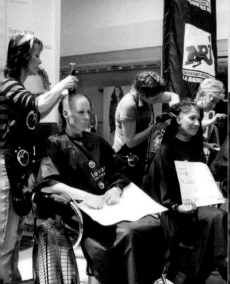

CANADIAN CHAMP

Just weeks after a good showing at the Boston Marathon, **Rob Watson** entered the Ottawa Marathon and was the top Canadian.

CUTTING TIME

Leanne Loney of Val-d'Or, Quebec finished her second marathon, but first in Ottawa. It was an "insanely magical experience," she says. "Ottawa will always hold a special place in my heart. It took having three kids to get me to be the runner I have always dreamed of being. When I finally made it to Ottawa in 2013, I was well-prepared, and beat my previous time by 23 minutes." And if running a marathon weren't enough for one day, after the race Loney drove to Gatineau and shaved her head at *Défi têtes rasées Leucan* to raise money for kids with cancer.

SPRING INTO THE FUTURE

Adidas launched the Springblade, its most expensive running shoe ever. The sneaker was dotted with 16 rounded, angled blades that were designed to work like angled springs that propel the runner forward when the springs bounce back.

EARS TO YOU

As he had done for several years, **Mark Wigmore** led the group of pace bunnies who guided runners through the marathon.

LATE NIGHT FODDER

Toronto Mayor **Rob Ford** became the subject of international news coverage and talk-show humour after admitting to smoking crack cocaine.

"We're not content to be smaller or medium-sized."

Tomorrow, the world

[AFTERWORD]

John Halvorsen is reluctant to set the kind of bold objectives that Jim Robinson established after taking over the helm of the Ottawa Marathon in 1996. And who can blame him? From fewer than 1,000 participants in 1994, the marathon has already grown to 7,000 entrants in 2014. In the past five years alone, the marathon has almost doubled in size.

And around the flagship race, Ottawa Race Weekend has blossomed into one of the largest running events in the world, with almost 50,000 registrants in 2014. That's almost 20 times the number of participants of 20 years ago.

Can the growth continue? Will it happen at the same rate? Halvorsen is cautiously optimistic.

"We've already come so far," he says. "If someone had told me a few years ago that we'd be at 7,000 and selling out in January, I wouldn't have believed it. Yet here we are."

Halvorsen has a long history with the event, going back to his days as an elite middle-distance runner. He won the 10k race in Ottawa four times, including a course record in 1988 that stood for more than 20 years. He represented his native Norway in the 1988 and 1992 Olympics.

After retiring from competition, he joined the board of Ottawa Race Weekend while working full-time in Ottawa's technology sector. After Robinson moved into semi-retirement, Halvorsen turned his passion into his new full-time job. Now it's up to him to lead and manage the growth of an event that is already thriving and expanding.

"The 10th largest marathon in North America last year had 7,000 runners in it," says Halvorsen. "So we're on the verge of getting in the top 10. Getting to 10,000 runners in the next few years is not out of the question. We have a chance to get ourselves into the top five or six marathons in North America."

For Halvorsen, it's not just about the numbers, but about building the marathon into a world-class event.

"It's being recognized as one of the major players," he says. "Cementing ourselves as a serious, top-league destination marathon. That means numbers, but it also means being well-organized, operating in a good city, and getting great support from the city."

Twenty years ago, the marathon lost most of its government support. Now there's an understanding that the event is good for Ottawa. Indeed, it attracts more tourists than almost any other event in the city.

The Ottawa Marathon will stay true to its roots of putting runners first, and follow through on Robinson's commitment to get the little details right. And the success of the event, Halvorsen says, will also be driven by the participation of elite runners.

"We will continue to have a world-class competitive event," he says. "That's part of the recognition. The marathons that have that status, that are part of that league, have a highly competitive event. That's part of elevating ourselves to that world level."

By aiming to be bigger and better, Halvorsen and his colleagues are rejecting any notion that Ottawa can't be a big player in an increasingly competitive market. He sees no reason why Ottawa can't be a continental and even global leader, with a bigger marathon than cities much larger in size.

"We're not the typical Ottawa group," he says. "We're not content to be smaller or medium-sized."

It's an attitude perfectly in keeping with the event itself. After all, marathons are about taking on the impossible, and, in the process, changing the way you look at yourself. Like a runner in training, the Ottawa Marathon has been built through hard work, and performed one step at a time. It has changed and improved not only the almost 100,000 runners who have crossed its finish line, but the city they have travelled across.

Acknowledgements

For 40 years, the Ottawa Marathon and Ottawa Race Weekend have been guided by a team whose professionalism is exceeded only by their devotion to providing runners with a unique and memorable experience every spring. I'm grateful for the support and direction provided by Joe Du Vall, John Halvorsen, Susan Marsh-Marconi, and Jim Robinson.

Dozens of participants, volunteers, and race officials from the past four decades have been a wonderful source of stories and photos. They are too many to name here, but I'm especially grateful to Ken Parker, whose passion for running impressed me long before I shared it; Martin Cleary, who shared his files from covering at least 30 Ottawa Marathons for the *Ottawa Citizen* and is deeply admired for his commitment to amateur sport, and Eleanor Thomas, whose memories and photographs of the marathon and Ottawa's running community in the 1970s and 1980s were invaluable. Thanks also to Marasport Photographic Productions and the *Ottawa Citizen* for so many of the pictures in this book.

Canada's Magnificent Marathon would not have been possible without the creativity, vision, and hard work of my two partners on this project, Lisa Georges and Sarah MacFadyen. As she always does, Lisa pulled together all the pieces of the puzzle into a visually appealing, coherent package. Sarah invested countless hours searching through archives, assembling submissions from runners, hunting down far-flung past participants, and tracking down photos.

Nothing I do is either possible or worthwhile without the love and support of my family. My wife Ginny and our children Erica, Jack, and Kate have given me a multitude of gifts that I treasure daily. I'm thankful for the support of my mother Florence and my in-laws Brian and Donna, all of whom entertained their grandchildren when book deadlines were approaching. And I'm always grateful for the example left by my father, John, who inspired my passion for the written word, and my sister, Dianne, with whom I shared a love of numbers.

My greatest source of inspiration for *Canada's Magnificent Marathon* was the incredible community of runners with whom I have shared a passion for the past dozen years. Perhaps Wally Herman said it best: "I never met a horse's ass in all those people." A race can be well-organized and follow a beautiful course, as Ottawa most certainly does. But it is nothing without the runners. The history of the Ottawa Marathon, wherever it is told, is their story.

[PHOTO INDEX]